AF291023

HEJI SHIN

THE BIG NUDES

CLARION

HEJI SHIN

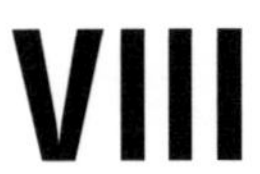

VIII

Contents

Curator's Note: A Pig Walks into a Bar...
Ebony L. Haynes

While preparing for *THE BIG NUDES*, Heji Shin called me and confidently announced, "It's going to be pigs." You can imagine my moment of hesitation. But moving past that, I knew there was something simultaneously amusing and unsettling about the idea. Shin's vision has always been directed toward pushing boundaries, making the familiar suddenly strange, and forcing us to reconsider how we engage with images. In many ways, Shin's pigs are the perfect extension of what Helmut Newton was doing with the female body in his *Big Nudes* series (Shin's inspiration for the show), where the unexpected subject leads the viewer to question everything.

Shin's exhibition was built around two major bodies of work, positioned in dialogue with each other in fascinating ways. First, richly printed in both color and black-and-white, are Shin's oversize, glossy photographs of pigs posed like fashion models. They recline seductively, arching their bodies in ways that immediately recall the famous poses of Newton's *Big Nudes*. The way Shin plays with the language of the fashion industry—the lighting, the slickness, the sense of allure—and applies it to these animals is deeply provocative. The pigs are cute, funny, strange, and disquieting, with uncannily humanlike bodies and skin. By taking on the subject of pigs, Shin invites us to come to our own conclusions and question the ways in which we're conditioned to respond to certain visual cues.

Then you turn to the second body of work: detailed scans, created with diffusion tensor imaging, a kind of MRI used for medical research, of the artist's own brain. The brain is the core of our identity, the physical organ that controls every aspect of who we are—our thoughts, feelings, memories. Those who can read the scans have unique access to Shin's interior, rendering her nude in an entirely new way. And yet when looked at as a series of images, the brain becomes an otherworldly, abstract landscape. It's a self-portrait that removes the face, removes the body, and shows us the innermost part of the subject in a way that is both revealing and mysterious. Shin takes this one step further by using the illusion technique known as Pepper's ghost to project a holographic 3-D image of her brain in the center of the gallery. It's a floating, pulsing, iridescent form, contained within a prism, that draws us in but also keeps us at a distance. It forces us to think about how much we rely on the visible to understand identity, and what happens when the immediately recognizable is stripped away, leaving only the traces of thought and consciousness.

Shin has built her reputation through immense consideration of composition, light, shape, and the various other formal qualities of an image, all while playing with the line between fashion, celebrity culture, and high art. She has always been interested in the idea of taste—what we consider beautiful, what we desire, what we find appropriate or taboo—and her work often makes us uncomfortably aware of our own voyeurism. In this volume of *Clarion*, Benoît Lamy de La Chapelle explores the context surrounding Shin's work, particularly power dynamics, symbolism, and the ways in which images are used to shape desire and identity.

Though Shin acknowledges that artists, like us all, are not free from their own motives and agendas, she prefers to approach the interpretation of her work as ambiguously as possible. After all, a joke isn't funny if you have to explain it. In *THE BIG NUDES*, Shin forces us to reckon with our own role as viewers—caught in the act of looking, or perhaps laughing, even when we're not quite sure what it is we're looking at.

Squealing like a Pig
Benoît Lamy de La Chapelle

There is a consensus, in many cultures, that being called a "pig" is an insult. The pig has held many contradictory positions across the globe since Roman times. In Heji Shin's *THE BIG NUDES*, showcasing large black-and-white and color portraits of young pigs, it is immediately obvious that the animals are utterly clean, though it would be misleading to suggest the artist's goal was to redeem the status of the hog. Shin's artistic endeavor in photographing animals has mainly been an effort to avoid the communal discourse around a certain species—its symbolism and meaning—in order to focus on the possibility of its use for other means, for both self-deprecating and provocative reasons.

As the title shows, Shin takes the 1981 exhibition and publication of Helmut Newton's *Big Nudes* as her point of departure for this project. One could say these artists have much in common: they are both German and both came to the United States to work; they are both photographers in the fashion industry, yet they do not draw a clear line between their commercial work and their artistic practices. Both intertwine these activities—not only does one finance the other, but each in turn nurtures the other formally and conceptually. This complication of genre not only gives form to a certain system of placing their figures but also allows the artists to reflect on how fashion iconography shapes the notion of desire, social behaviors, and power relationships. While Newton limited his endeavor to a glamorous, erotic chic, Shin goes further into the sexual and pornographic dimension of the nude. Shin has always been impressed by the radicalness of Newton's *Big Nudes*, for the impression of power the series conveys regarding the nude woman, where she is depicted as the person in charge rather than the submissive object of male sexual pleasure. As the art-historical tradition of the odalisque shows—for example François Boucher's *Resting Girl (Jeune fille allongée,* 1751)—many Western artists have painted young women who were either prostitutes or courtesans, in doing so exploring their own sexual fantasies (and inviting viewers to take pleasure in the same desires). Newton's series helped to create the mythology

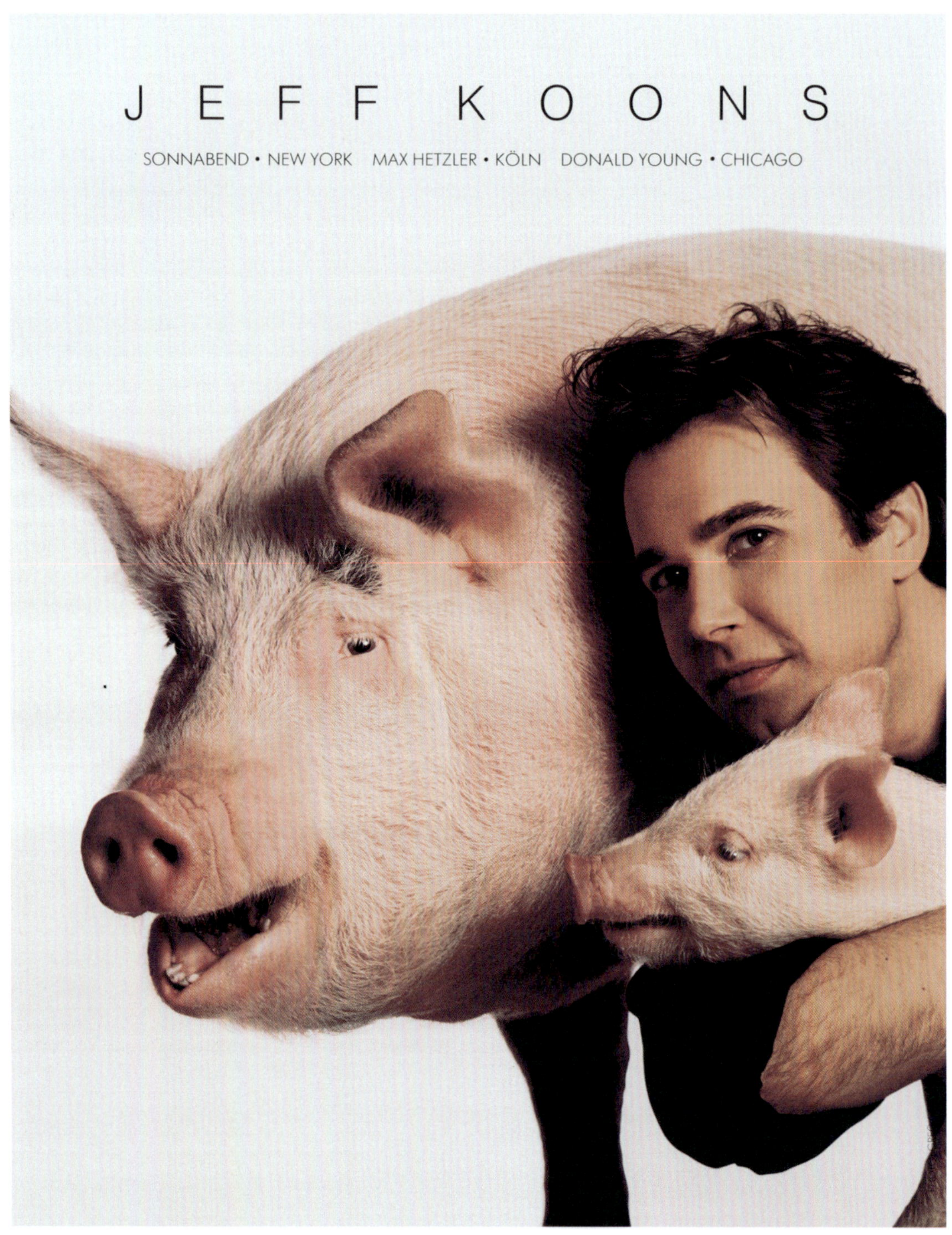

Advertisement by Jeff Koons, published in
Flash Art, November/December 1988

of the single, independent working woman of the 1980s, who equaled men intellectually and physically; this vision has since shifted toward the popular cliché of the strong woman as dominatrix, providing new libidinal excitement and pleasure for men. The photographs also aided in establishing the aesthetic criteria for the tall, slender supermodels of the late 1980s and early 1990s, shaping Western standards of beauty that reverberate to this day.

It is not necessarily the aspect of feminist empowerment present in Newton's work that motivated Shin to appropriate it; she simply liked the look and sculptural presence of those intimidating nude women. In a blasphemous gesture, blended with her sharp sense of humor, Shin allowed herself to touch an untouchable icon, replacing the celebrated glamorous young woman with a pig—the last subject an advocate of good taste would expect to see in an artwork. This is one of the reasons Jeff Koons included the pig in many of his sculptural works, as well as in *Art Ad* (1988; p. 10), an advertisement for his exhibition *Banality* at Sonnabend Gallery in New York. Here Koons appears against a white background, smiling at the camera from between two pigs. Shin's pig portraits certainly share their sense of provocation and their commercial aesthetic choices with Koons's ad; her photographs would require only a slogan to function as commercial work. In the gallery space, Shin's huge framed prints force distance on the viewer, and though some are black-and-white, others are in color, the bright pink of the pigs' bare flesh evoking human skin, bringing an erotic aspect to the fore. As in George Orwell's 1945 novel *Animal Farm*, Shin's pigs replace human beings to highlight one of the worst sides of humanity: the desire to hide our true perversity behind puritanism or hypocritical repression.

In comparison to Shin's previous photographic work, these images mark the artist's most indirect take on pornography. Usually, she prefers to get straight to the point, creating more immediately affecting images. In her early series *Make Love* (2011), essentially a sex education book for German teenagers, Shin's forthright tendency was already biting. *Poor in World* (2012) bluntly admits the intimate bonds between capital and sex—or rather, the power of capital to turn anyone into a prostitute. In *#lonelygirl* (2016; p. 12, top), Shin photographed a funny-looking monkey playing with a dildo against a pink background, focusing on its ass, while *Mating* (2018) presents a dark X-ray image of two dogs having sex.

Calling someone a "pig" undeniably carries the intention to humiliate and degrade. It also recalls Shin's series *Men Photographing Men* (2018; p. 12, bottom), as "pigs" is one of the numerous pejorative words applied to the police. In this series, the nude subject is inverted from women to men, in photographs that depict gay porn actors dressed as policemen and engaged in sexual intercourse. The scenes can be quite shocking or crude to viewers not familiar with a universe in which tools of repression—guns, swords, billy clubs, handcuffs, flashlights—and sexual organs are exhibited together, foregrounding an unexpected visual violence. This feeling is heightened by a sense of uncertainty regarding what is really happening in this series, an ambiguity that flirts with the taboo of male rape in Western society, which remains barely audible in the current mass-media broadcast. The shock provoked by this series is reminiscent of another unbearable visual experience: the rape scene in John Boorman's 1972 film *Deliverance*. Here, the "big nude" is the actor Ned Beatty, forced to undress and "squeal like a pig," carrying the weight and the representation of extreme male violence in a disastrous moment. This is another possible interpretation of Shin's ambiguous pigs, whose bare presence surrounds and overwhelms visitors in *THE BIG NUDES*.

According to Camille Paglia's controversial book *Sexual Personae*, "amorality, aggression, sadism, voyeurism, and pornography" have always been present in art, even though this subject matter has "been ignored or glossed over by most academic critics," therefore denying great art its sexual orientation.[1] Because pop culture has for decades merged with art, it is now the principal vehicle for pornographically oriented content in everyday life. Shin's pigs underline today's pornographic environment, be it advertising,

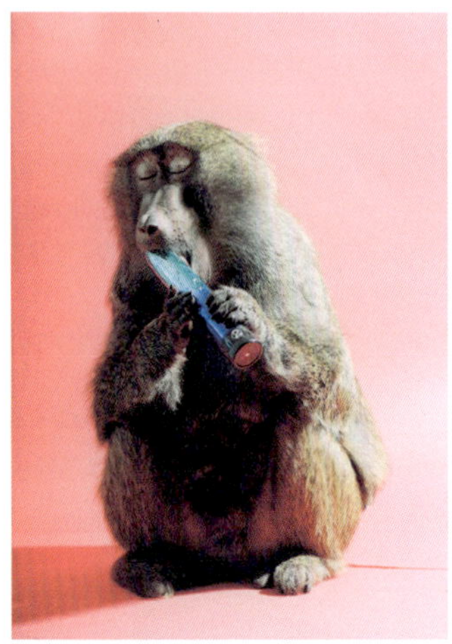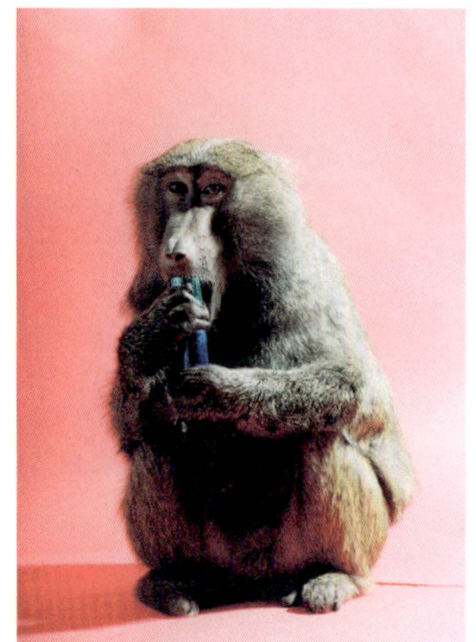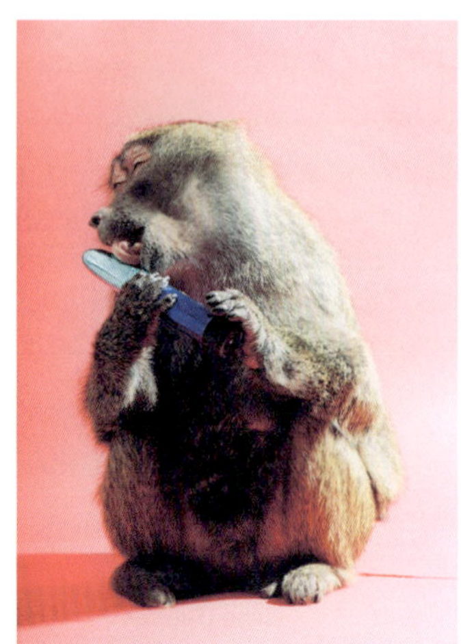

Heji Shin, *#lonelygirl*, 2016
Inkjet print on archival paper, each: 22 ¼ × 17 ¼ inches | 56.5 × 43.8 cm

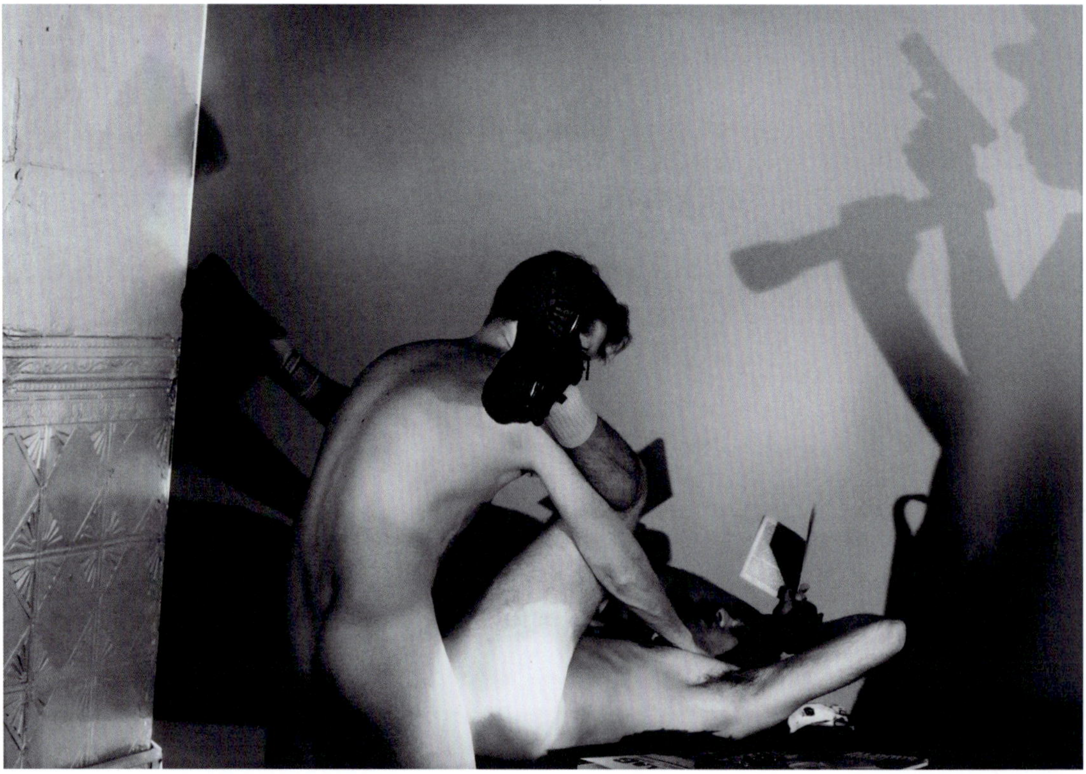

Heji Shin, *We Live in a Society*, 2018
Inkjet print, 31 ¼ × 43 ½ inches | 79.4 × 110.5 cm

cinema, social media, free online porn, or fashion and design. This reality has been aptly coined "pharmacopornographic" by the thinker Paul B. Preciado for its all-encompassing power over our media-driven and medically led society:

> Pharmacopornographic control infiltrates and dominates the entire flow of capital, from agrarian biotechnology to high-tech industries of communication. . . . In this period of the body's technomanagement, the pharmacopornographic industry synthesizes and defines a specific mode of production and consumption, a masturbatory temporization of life, a virtual and hallucinogenic aesthetic of the living object, an architecture that transforms inner space into exteriority and the city into interiority and "junkspace" by means of mechanisms of immediate auto-surveillance and ultrarapid diffusion of information, a continuous mode of desiring and resisting, of consuming and destroying, of evolution and self-destruction.[2]

Such control would be easy to avoid were it not ubiquitous, dominating (consider Shin's decision to reproduce her pigs at sizes larger than life) and sneaking into every detail of our lives. Professional fashion photography and amateur content production, both of which we encounter routinely on social media, contain a multitude of hidden codes insinuating how one should behave, feel, and look. Social media platforms that make each user a brand—or a potential one—employ every possible pop-culture message to, in turn, sell other brands: "We are certainly still confronting a form of social control, but this time it's a matter of *control lite*, a bubbly type of control, full of colors and wearing Mickey Mouse ears and the Brigitte Bardot low-cut look, as opposed to the cold, disciplinary architecture of the panoptic illustrated by Foucault."[3]

Controlling the masses through pop culture, entertainment, media, and the internet (where everyone is a consumer, a producer, a judge, and a victim all at once) is certainly one of the best ways to wield power. *THE BIG NUDES* raises a question about the ways "artists" (not necessarily just fine artists working on their art, but also artists working for a living—graphic designers, creatives in the commercial realm, and so on) are involved in the making of the mind, from the early days of propaganda to the present. For all the ways late capitalism has become all-encompassing and inescapable, the old topic of the complicit artist's responsibility has become quite quaint. From mainstream fashion commissions to cutting-edge art, Shin's photographic work underlines how artists participate in making updated and subtle forms of propaganda. In 1975, the artist Sarah Charlesworth clearly broke the romantic view of the artist, "neutral or independent of material conditions":

> For each of us there is a certain element of contradiction involved in the majority of personal and professional choices that we make, a certain tension between self survival/self interest and social interest/species survival. Some of us feel this conflict more intensely than others and we have varying interests and values at stake. It is important, however, that we begin to recognize and elucidate the criteria and implications of choice rather than continue to apologize, rationalize, and obfuscate. None of us, neither artist, critic, dealer, curator, nor "patron of the arts," can be said to be free of conflict of interest when it comes to the making of the cultural phenomena "art."[4]

By showing the true face of late capitalism and the degree to which artists are always involved in it (whether they like it or not), Shin indicates to her viewers how we are being fooled, if not fucked. Since it is through pleasure and comfort that control is wielded and reinforced, "artists" are the precarious subordinates of a system that uses high-tech propaganda to convince citizens of the rationality of its absurd and incoherent policies. By referencing Orwell's *Animal Farm* in her choice of subject, Shin evokes the governing body that relies on lies to establish power over its people. In *THE BIG NUDES*, the pigs look down at us from above, sometimes recalling the cute titular character from the 1995 film *Babe*, at other times appearing to laugh at us. Because of their surprisingly human faces, they can come across as frightening, too. Looking from photograph to

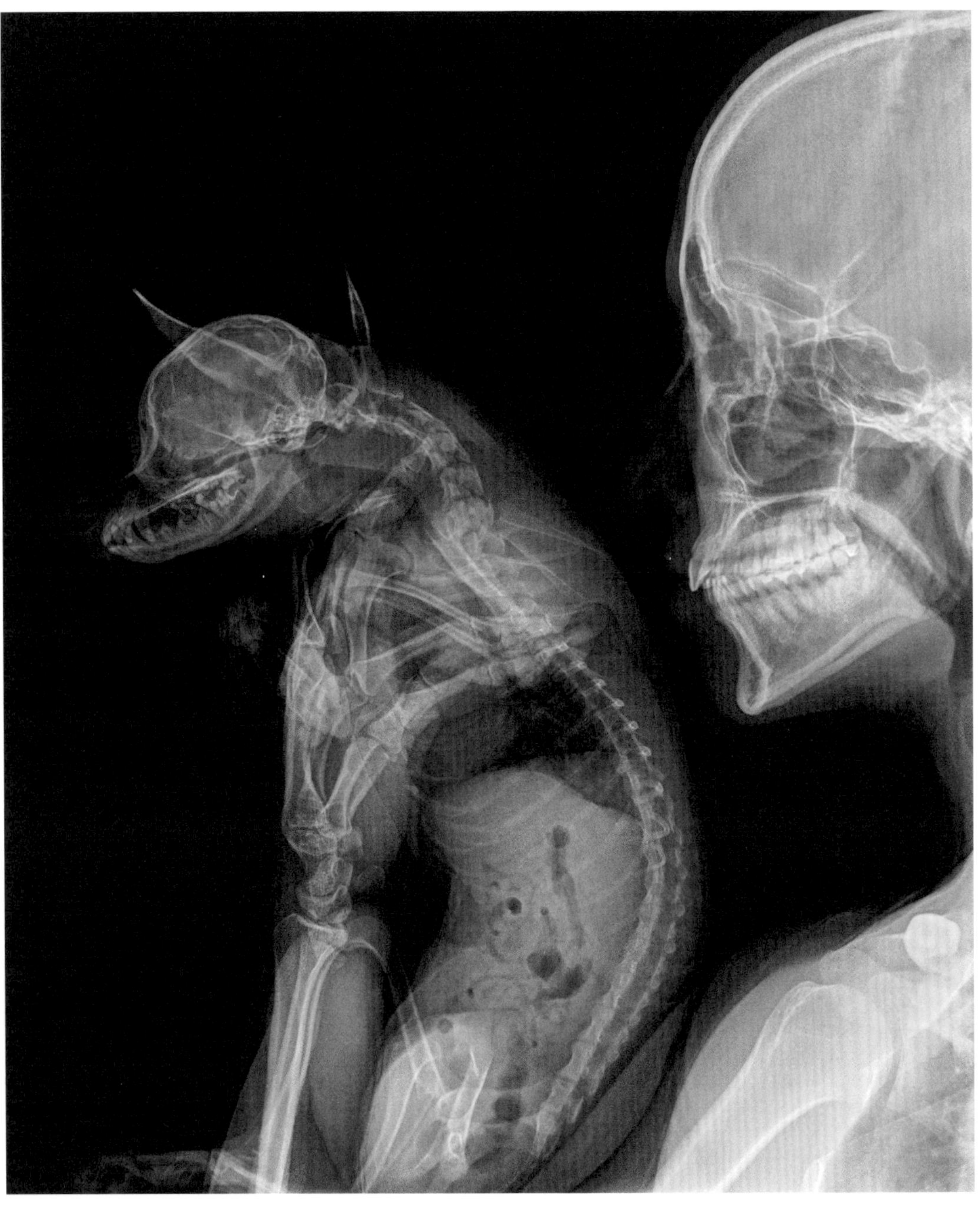

Heji Shin, *Self-Portrait Holding a Chihuahua II*, 2018
Inkjet print on aluminium, 28 ½ × 23 ⅜ inches | 72.5 × 59.5 cm

photograph, taking in the subjects' various poses, viewers find themselves caught in an ambiguous loop. The feeling of entrapment is conjured by the space: a closed room where the pigs surround us, observing us with their dubious glances, seeming as if they are friendly, as much as they could devour us.

The arrangement of the photographs recalls the architecture of the panopticon, which the presence of a glass pyramid in the center of the room further emphasizes. Here, viewers are invited to move around a holographic scan of the artist's brain. *THE BIG NUDES* thus exhibits both traditional and more recent, high-tech forms of control. According to Michel Foucault's concept of biopolitics,[5] Gilles Deleuze's "society of control,"[6] and Preciado's pharmacopornography, this control does not stop at the skin's surface—as might be suggested by the clear presence of the pigs' flesh—but slips deep inside the body and the mind. The enlarged scans of the artist's brain (*Big Nude I, II,* and *III*; pp. 55, 35, and 69), hung among the portraits of swine, somehow corroborates the medical turn of control theorized by Preciado. Shin's work stands at the precise point where paranoia meets the development of mass surveillance. She makes it obvious that political trope and truth are two separate things, and that governments, leading their citizens away from the truth—Does anyone even know what truth is anymore?—through propaganda and lies is precisely what keeps democracy going in our age of post-truth. "The naked truth," we used to say.

Throughout the history of figurative painting and photography, artists have turned to the genre of the self-portrait to present to the world their explorations of the self. In photography, for example, consider Nadar's *Self-Portrait in Twelve Poses* (*Autoportrait en douze poses*, 1861–1867), Gisèle Freund's *Self-Portrait with Rolleiflex* (*Autoportrait au Rolleiflex*, 1952), Vivian Maier's shop window self-portraits (c. 1950s–1970s), and even Newton's *Self Portrait with Wife and Models* (1981). So far, Shin has shied away from traditional self-portraiture. Rather, she prefers to take a different path, to experiment with alternative depictions of self. In *THE BIG NUDES*, her most readable endeavors

into the genre are *Big Nude I, II,* and *III*. Though the revealing of the physical matter of her brain would seem to be quite intrusive, Shin herself remains unidentifiable, invisible. The same is true of the holograph itself (2023; pp. 38–43): the more one attempts to penetrate this three-dimensional representation of Shin's brain, the more abstract it becomes, blurring its reality. This can also be said of Shin's earlier series of self-portraits of her holding dogs (2018; p. 14), in which we encounter radiographs of the artist's skull, but no trace of her face. Though the pig portraits and the medical scans displayed in *THE BIG NUDES* are distinct bodies of work, Shin considers the two "genetically related."[7] Throughout her career—from the series of camels in *Camp Habibi* (2013) to the monkey in *#lonelygirl*—Shin has resolved the issue of self-portraiture by considering her animal subjects as surrogates for herself.[8] Despite their differences, these animals are always funny looking, creatures that make the viewer want to smile, if not laugh. This gives Shin some distance from the solemnity of self-representation, allowing her to deal with this unavoidable genre with humor and providing her a way out of the overwhelming and suffocating presence of self-portraiture in our connected society—the poor image we call "the selfie."

A pig as a self-portrait: Could it be that Shin's photographic work is mere provocation? Regardless of everything her disruptive photographs bring to mind, she belongs to a generation of artists for whom subversion in art has become a thing of the past, despite the expanding expectation for it among contemporary artists—a cliché continuously used in the mass media to qualify contemporary art, from the Young British Artists to Maurizio Cattelan. In my mind, Shin's seemingly simple gesture of photographing pigs aims to leave the viewer in a void of interpretation. In *THE BIG NUDES*, the pig is not necessarily a provocation toward good taste. Through her feigned disinterest in the symbolism of pigs, Shin questions the prevalence of nudity, porn, and violence today, as well as the things humans do to others, and to themselves, within the realms of politics, science, and representation.

Notes

1 Camille Paglia, *Sexual Personae: Art and Decadence from Nefertiti to Emily Dickinson* (New Haven: Yale University Press, 1990), p. viii.

2 Paul B. Preciado, *Testo Junkie: Sex, Drugs, and Biopolitics in the Pharmacopornographic Era* (New York: The Feminist Press, 2013), pp. 40–41.

3 Preciado, *Testo Junkie*, p. 211.

4 Sarah Charlesworth, "A Declaration of Dependence," *The Fox* 1, no. 1 (1975), p. 3.

5 See Michel Foucault, *The Birth of Biopolitics: Lectures at the Collège de France, 1978–1979* (New York: Picador, 2010).

6 See Gilles Deleuze, "Postscript on Control Societies," in Deleuze, *Negotiations, 1972–1990*, trans. Martin Joughin (New York: Columbia University Press, 1995).

7 Heji Shin, *THE BIG NUDES*, video, https://52walker.com/exhibitions/heji-shin-the-big-nudes.

8 *#lonelygirl* press release, Galerie Bernhard, Zurich, 2016, https://galeriebernhard.com/exhibitions/heji-shin-lonelygirl.

PLATES

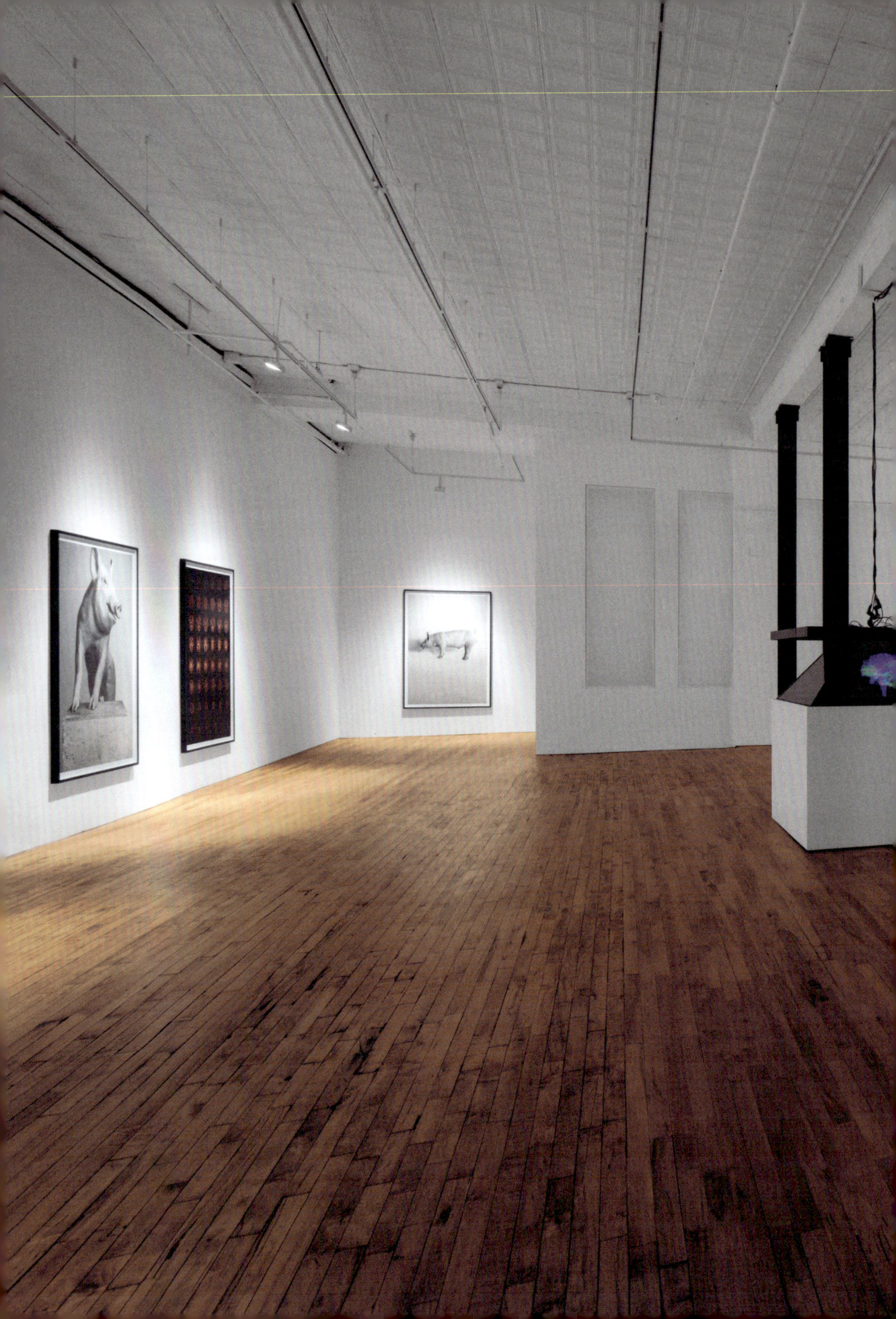

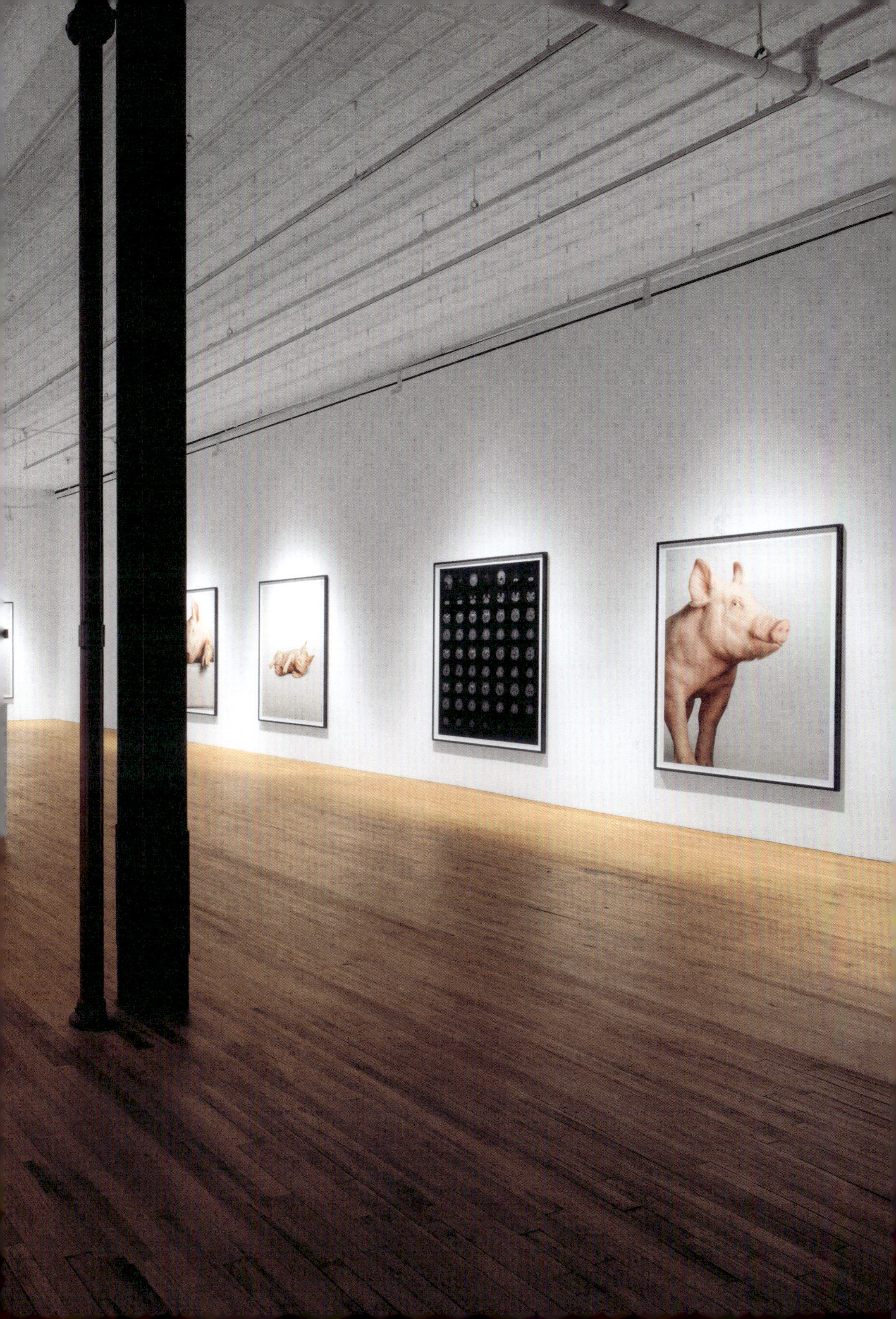

You've come a long way, baby!, 2023

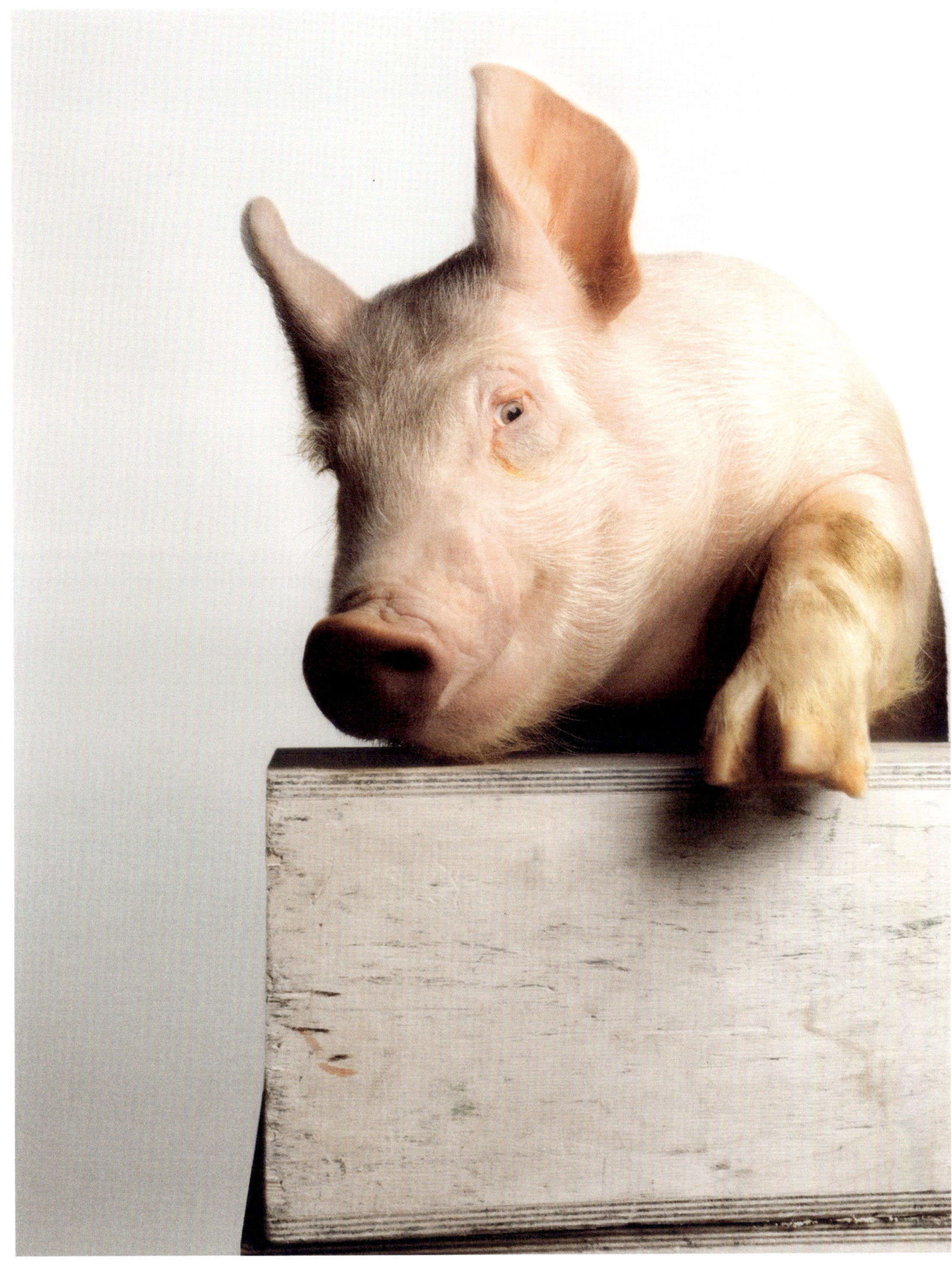

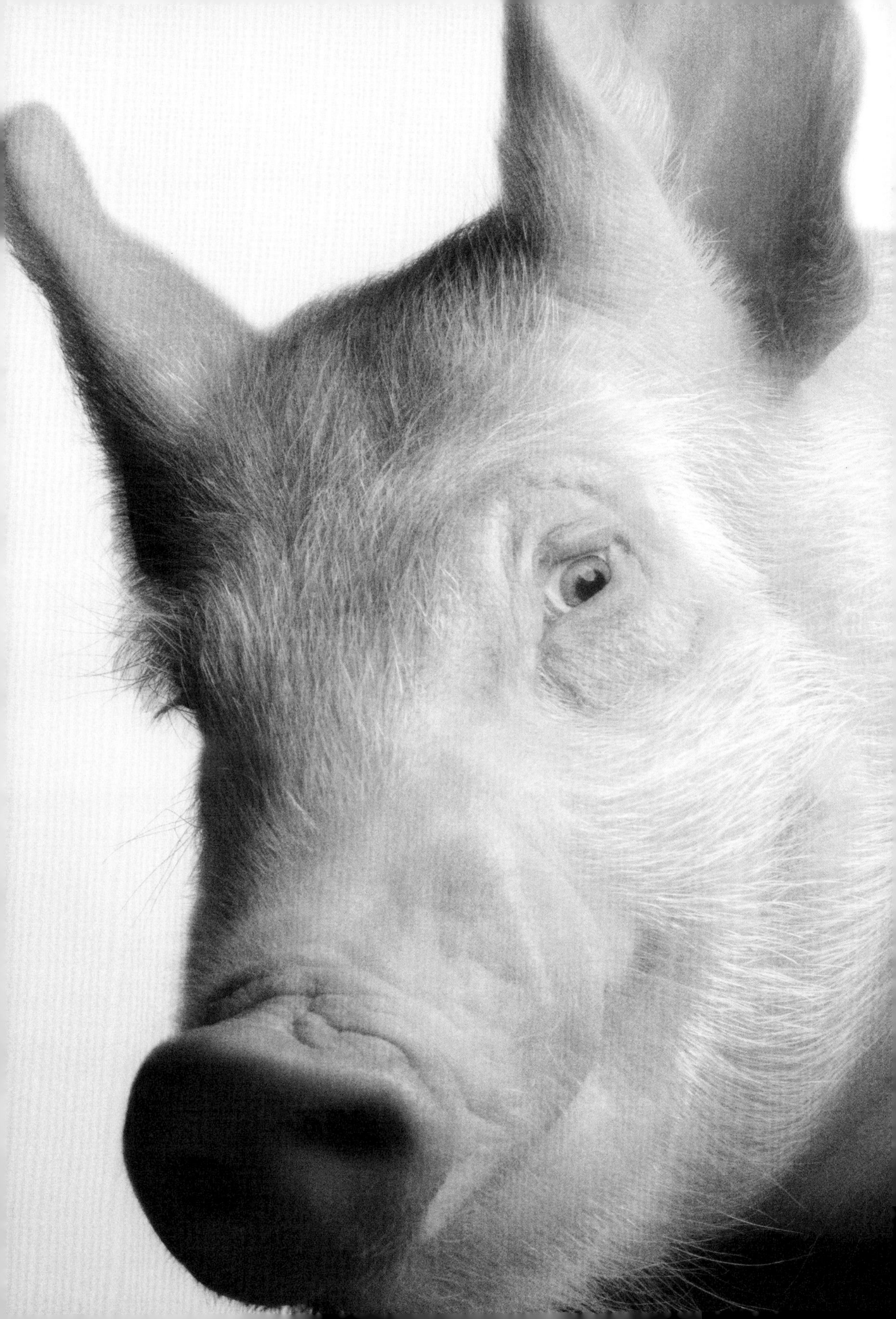

Reclining Nude, 2023

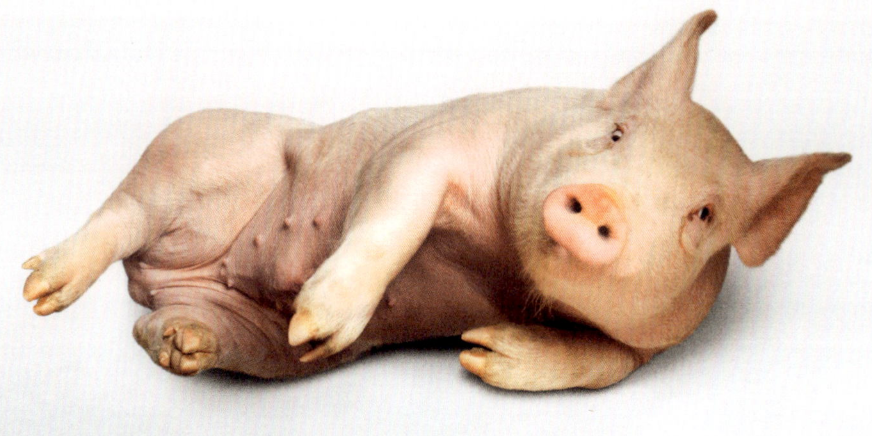

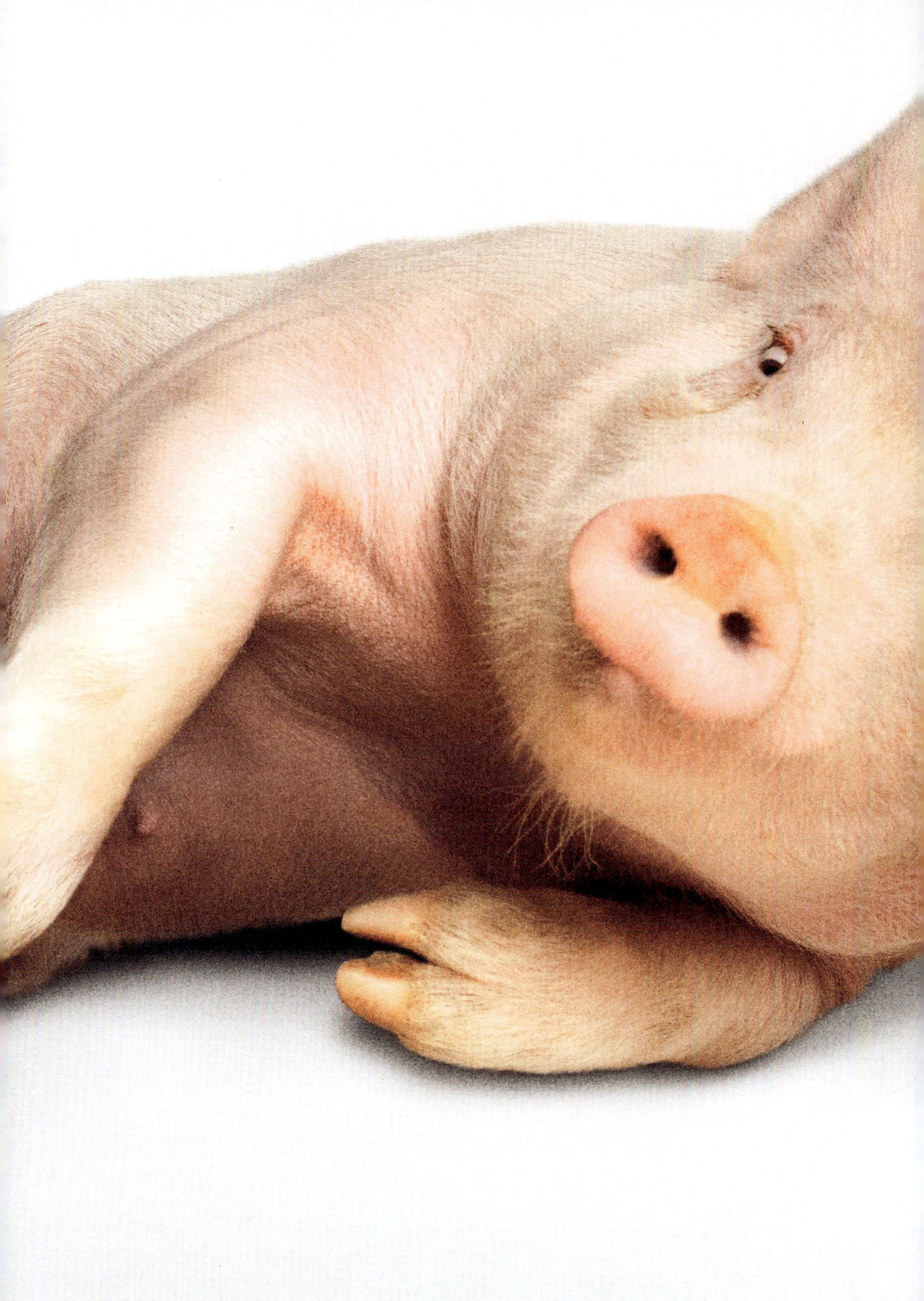

Eat Me, 2023

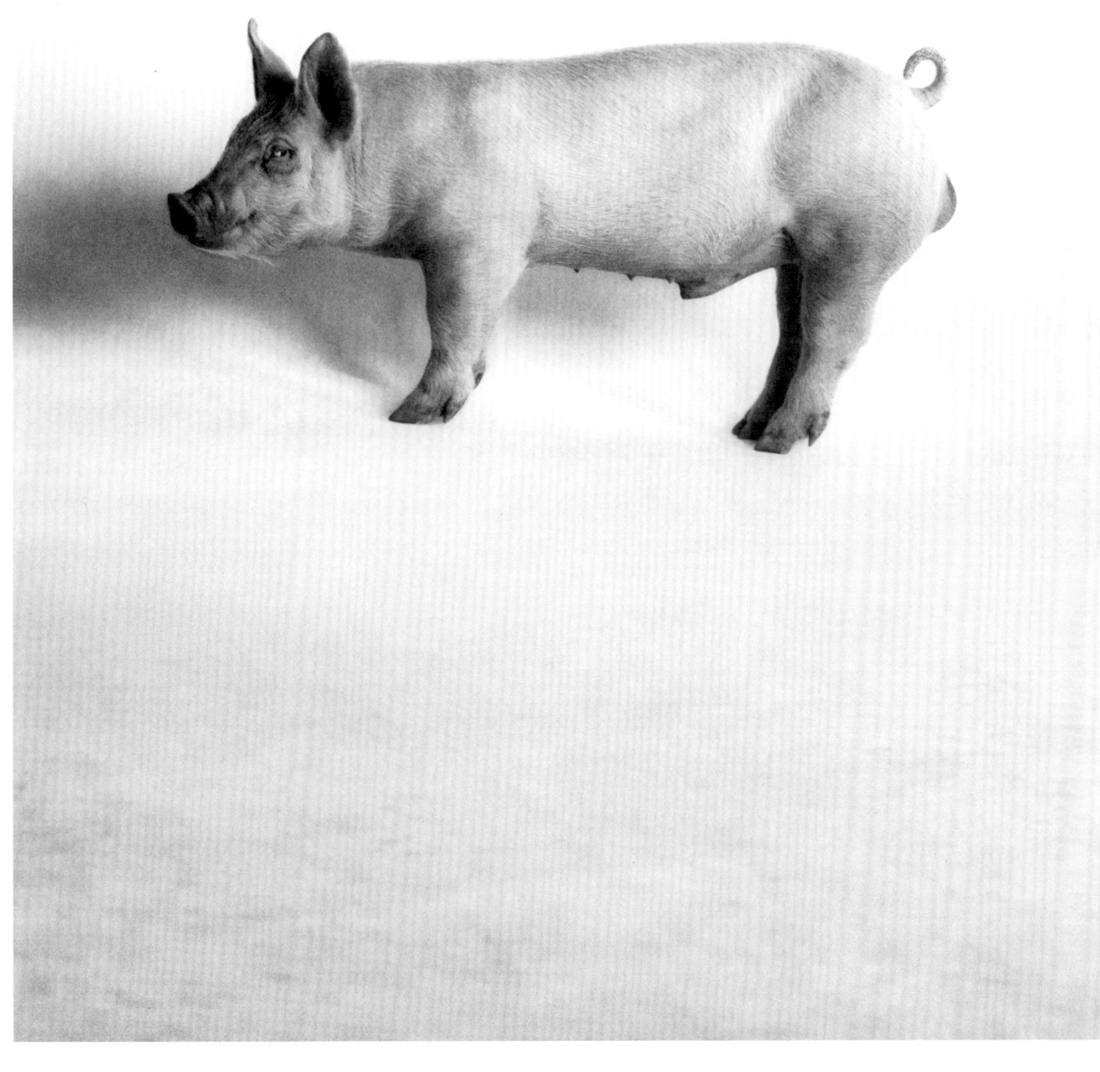

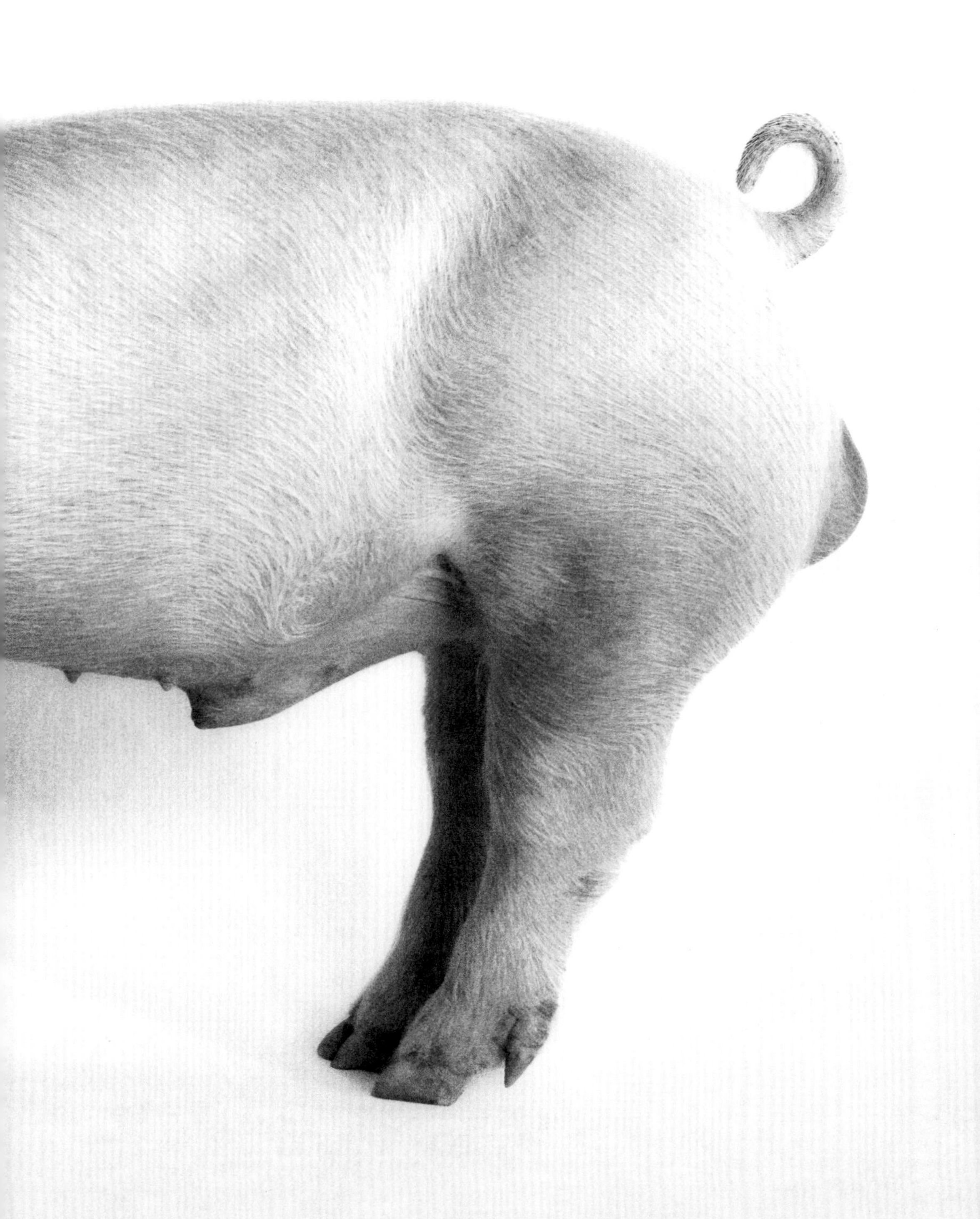

Big Nude II, 2023

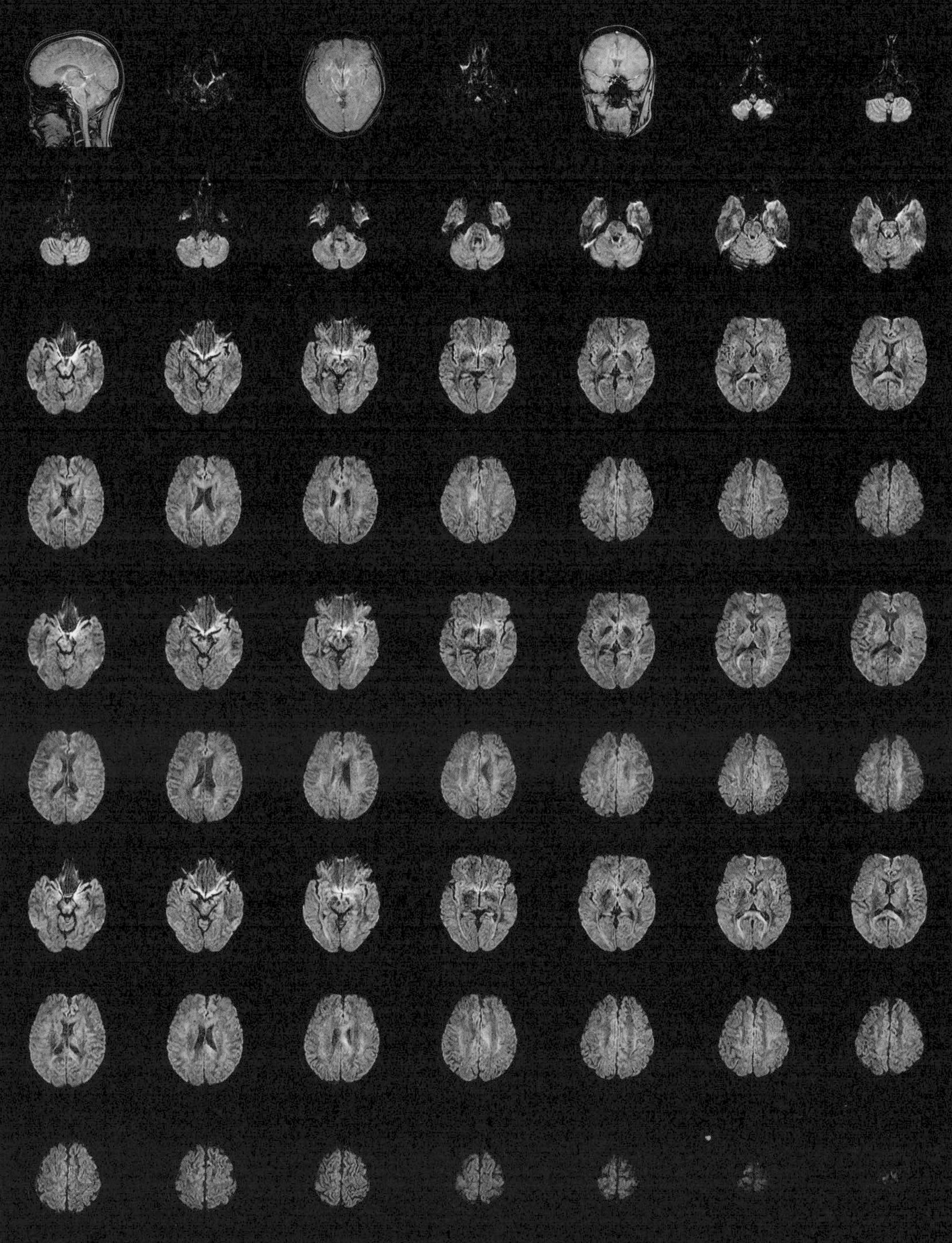

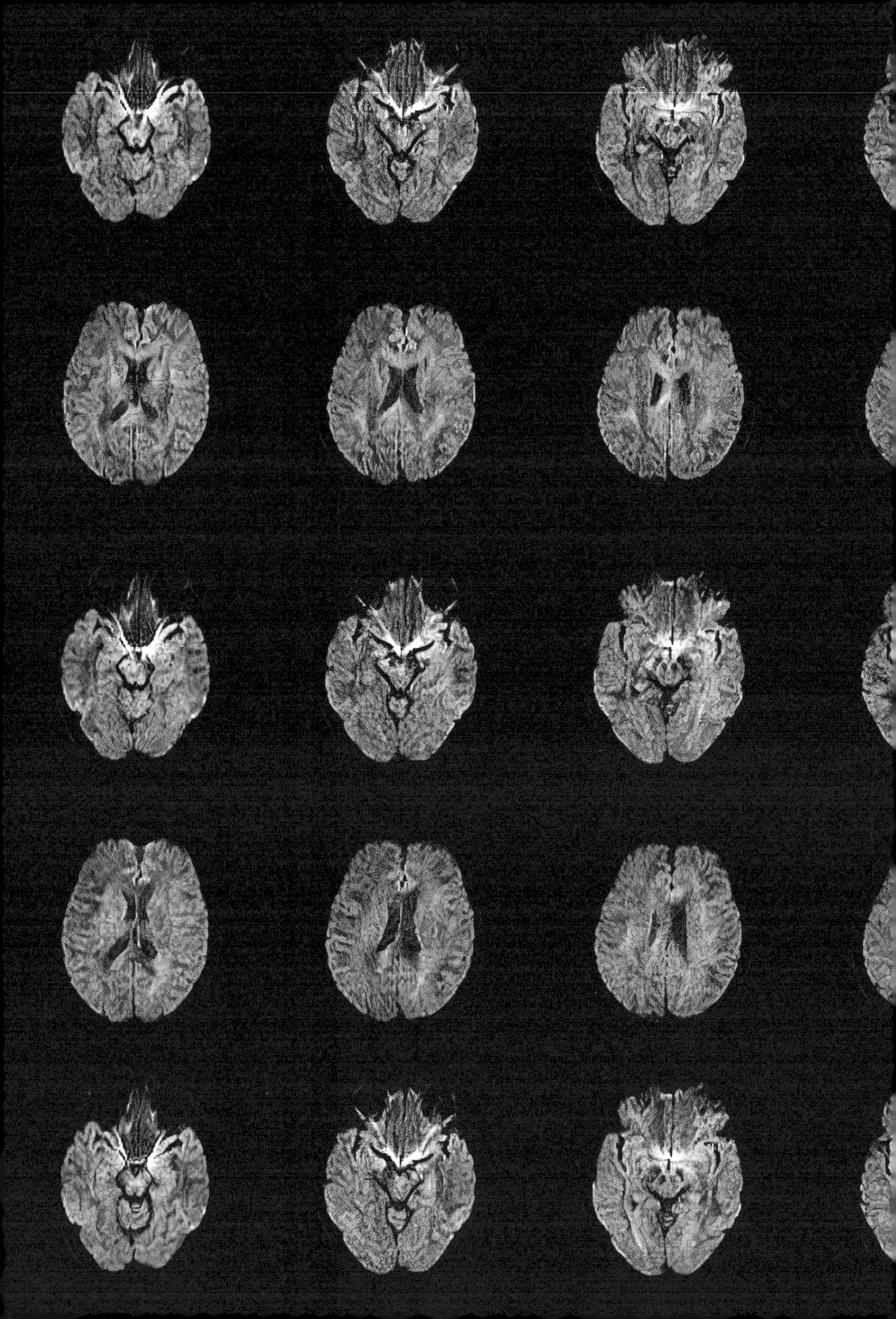

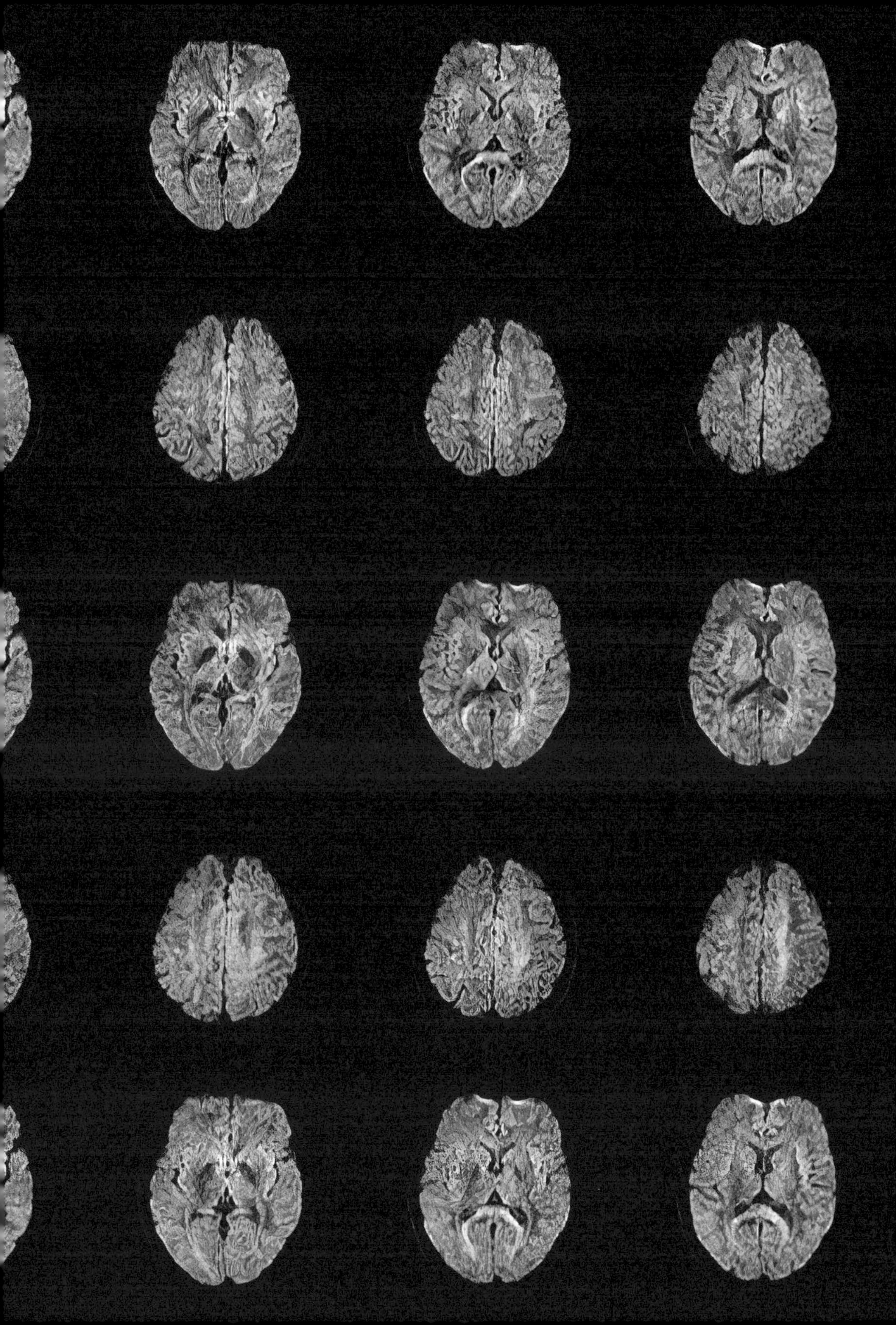

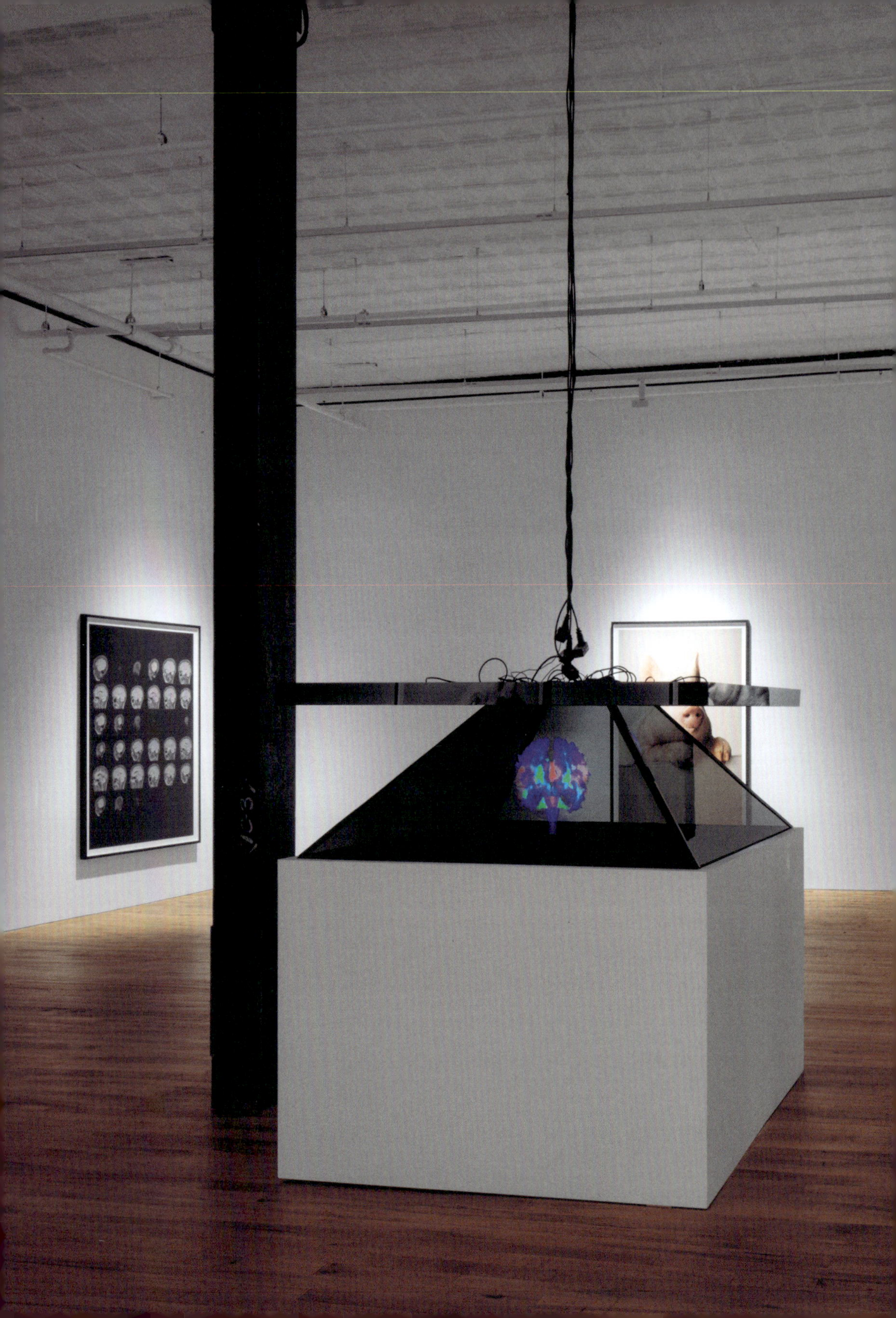

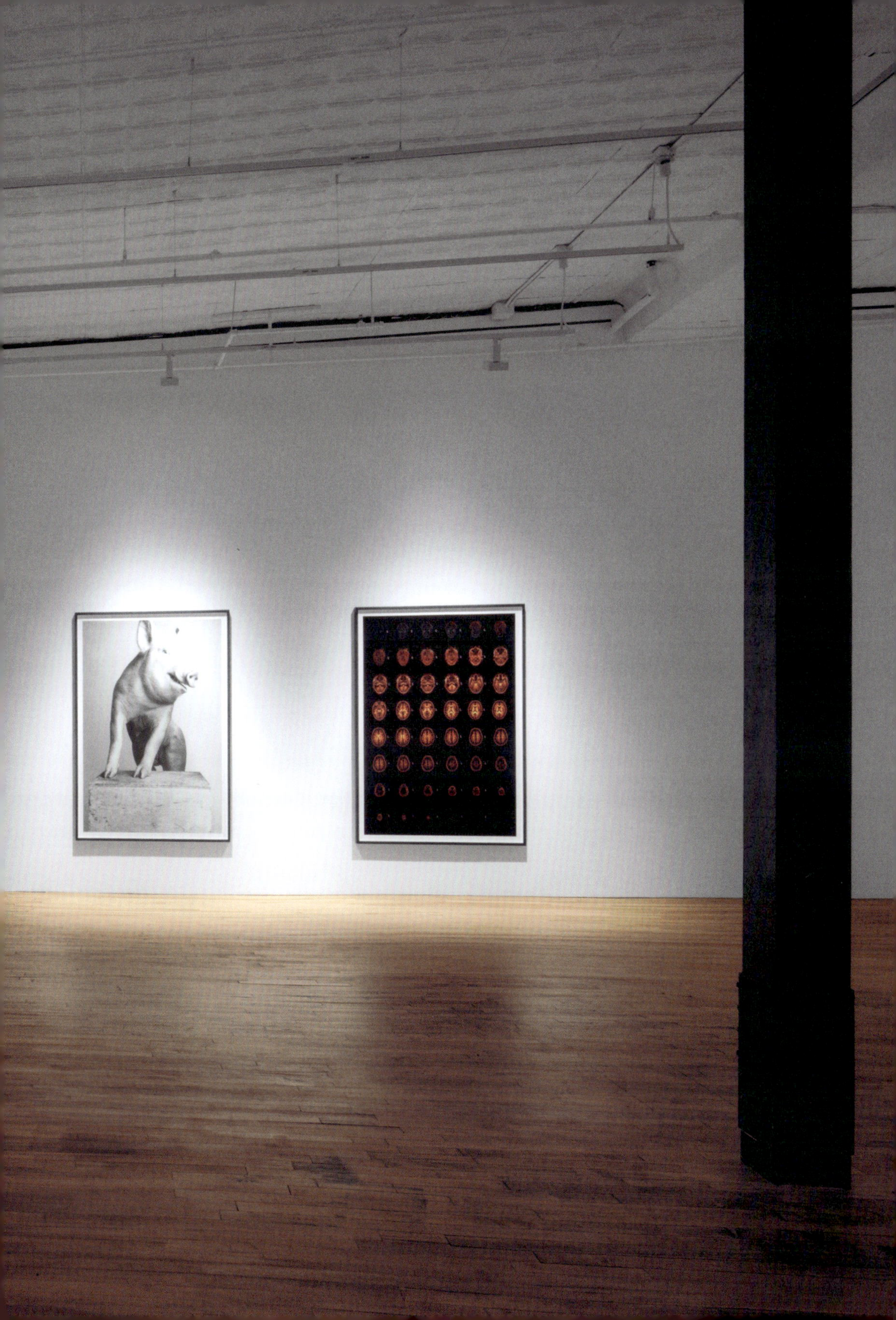

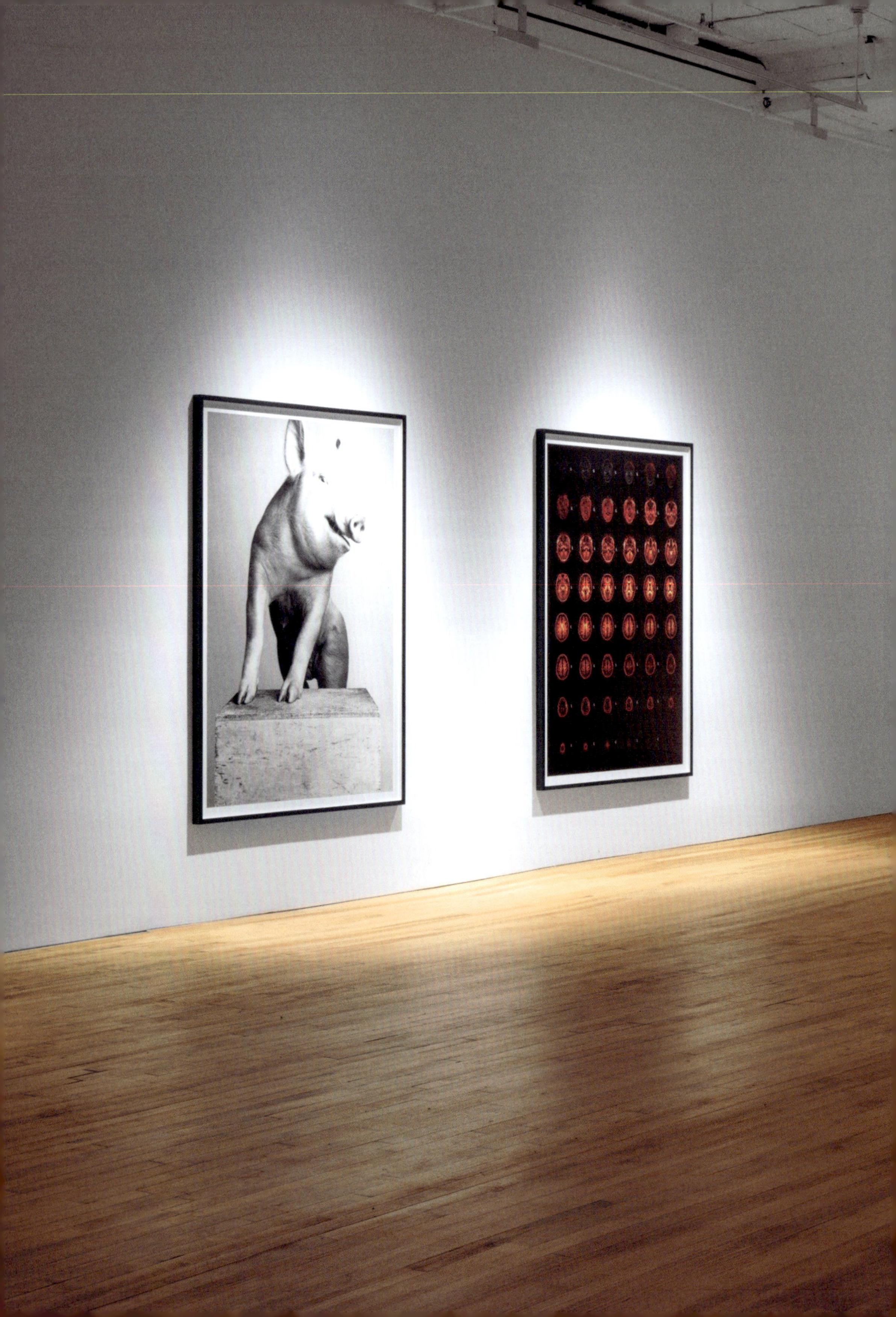

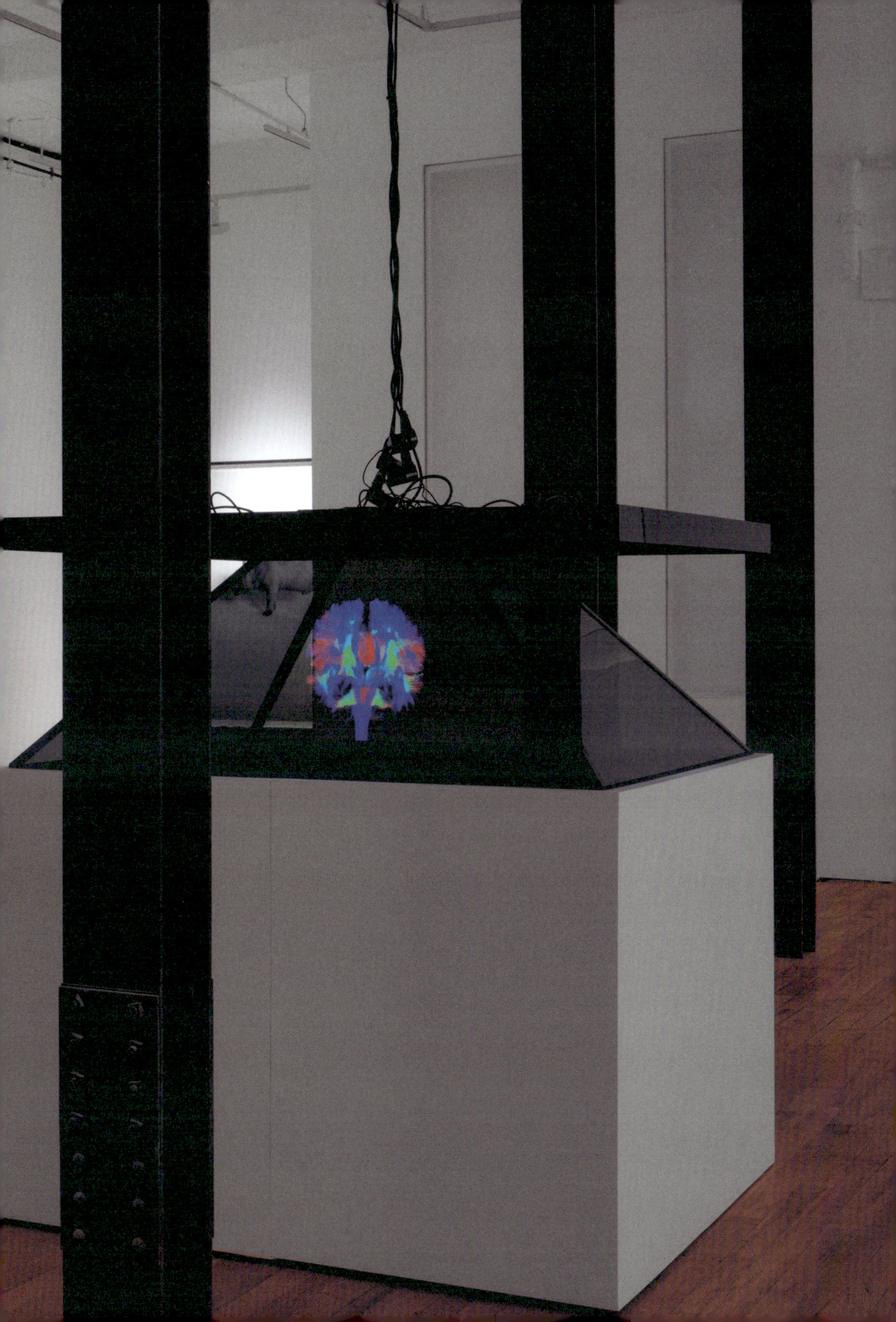

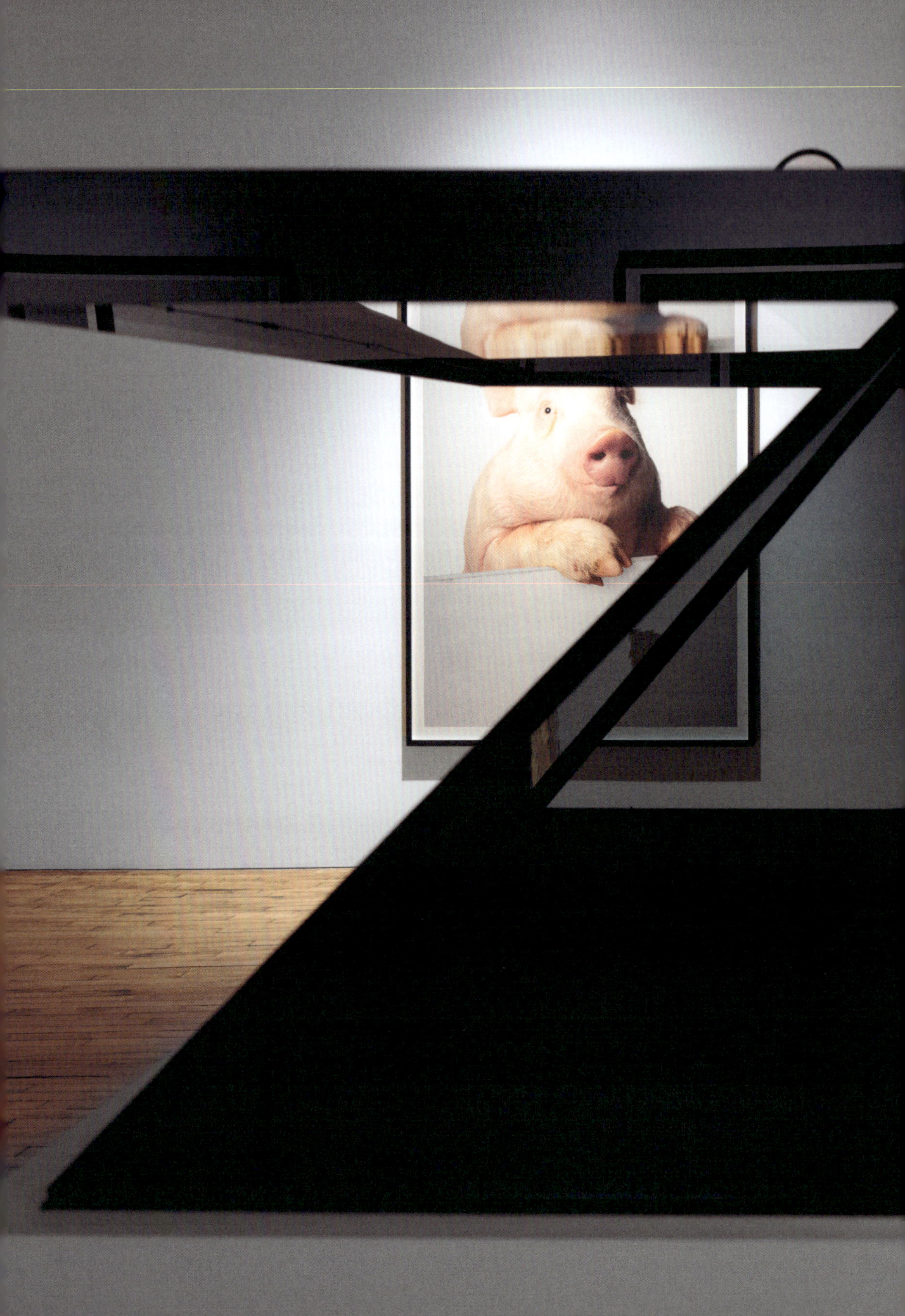

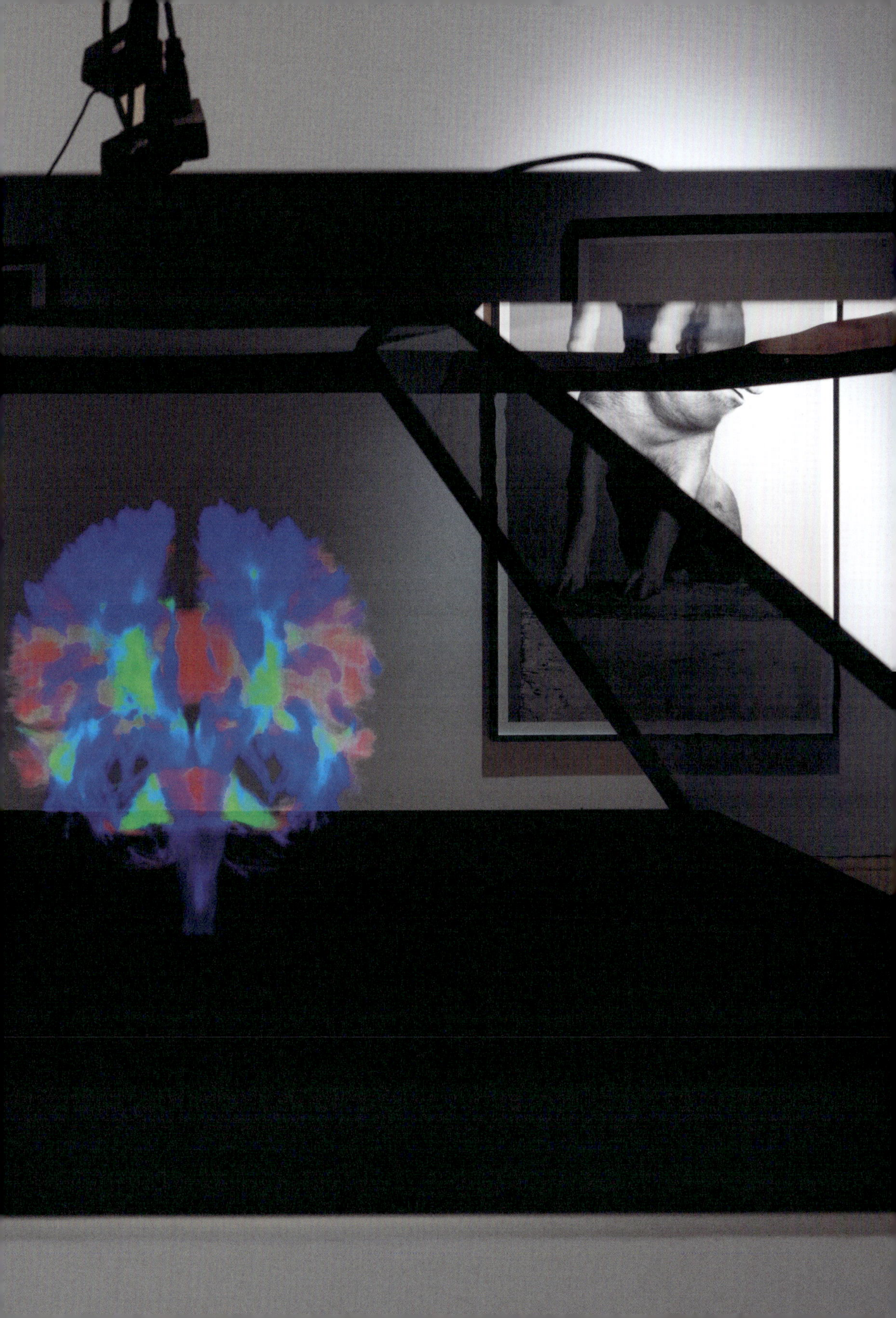

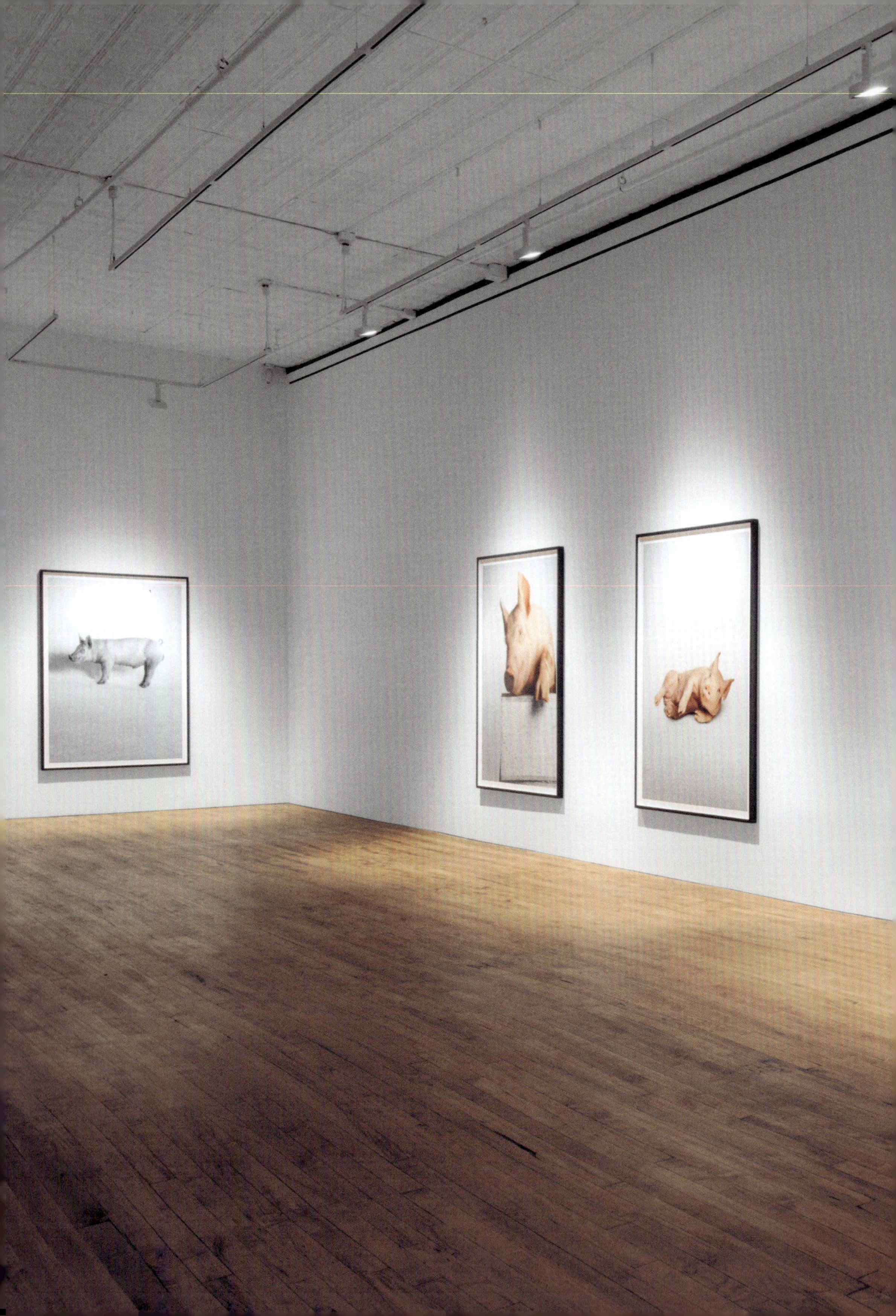

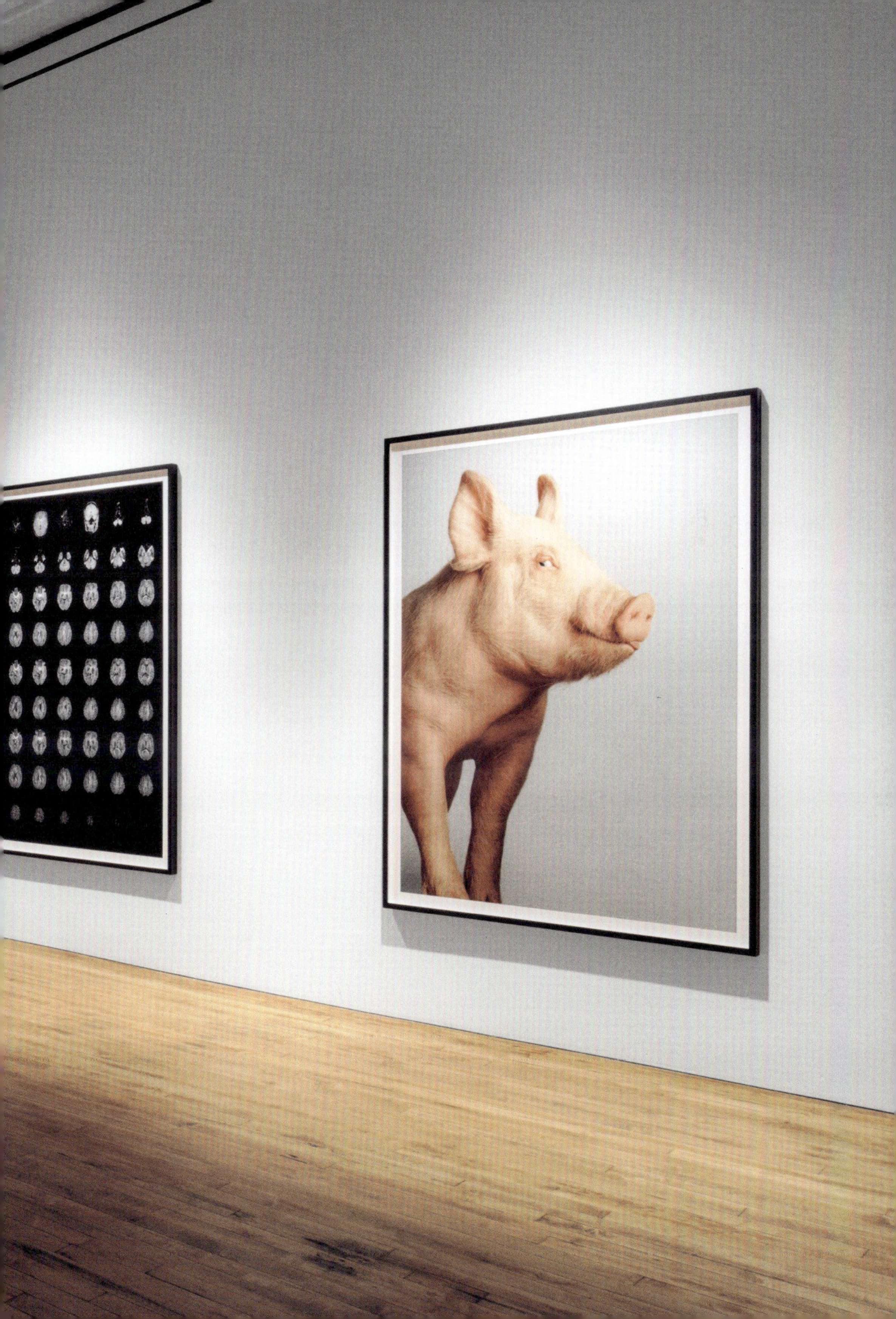

Opposite: *Sloth*, 2023

Pages 38–43:
Untitled, 2023

Opposite: *Sloth*, 2023

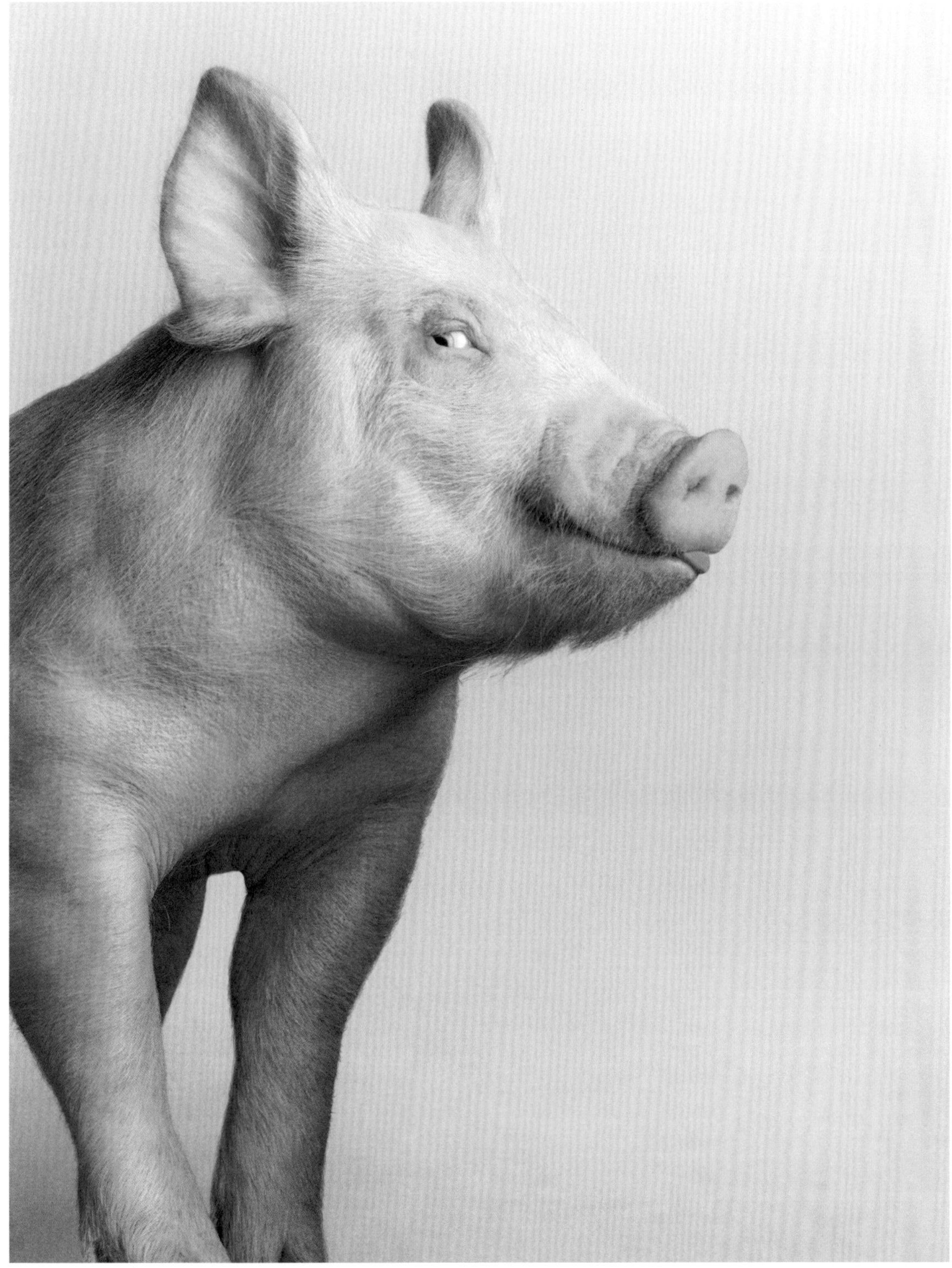

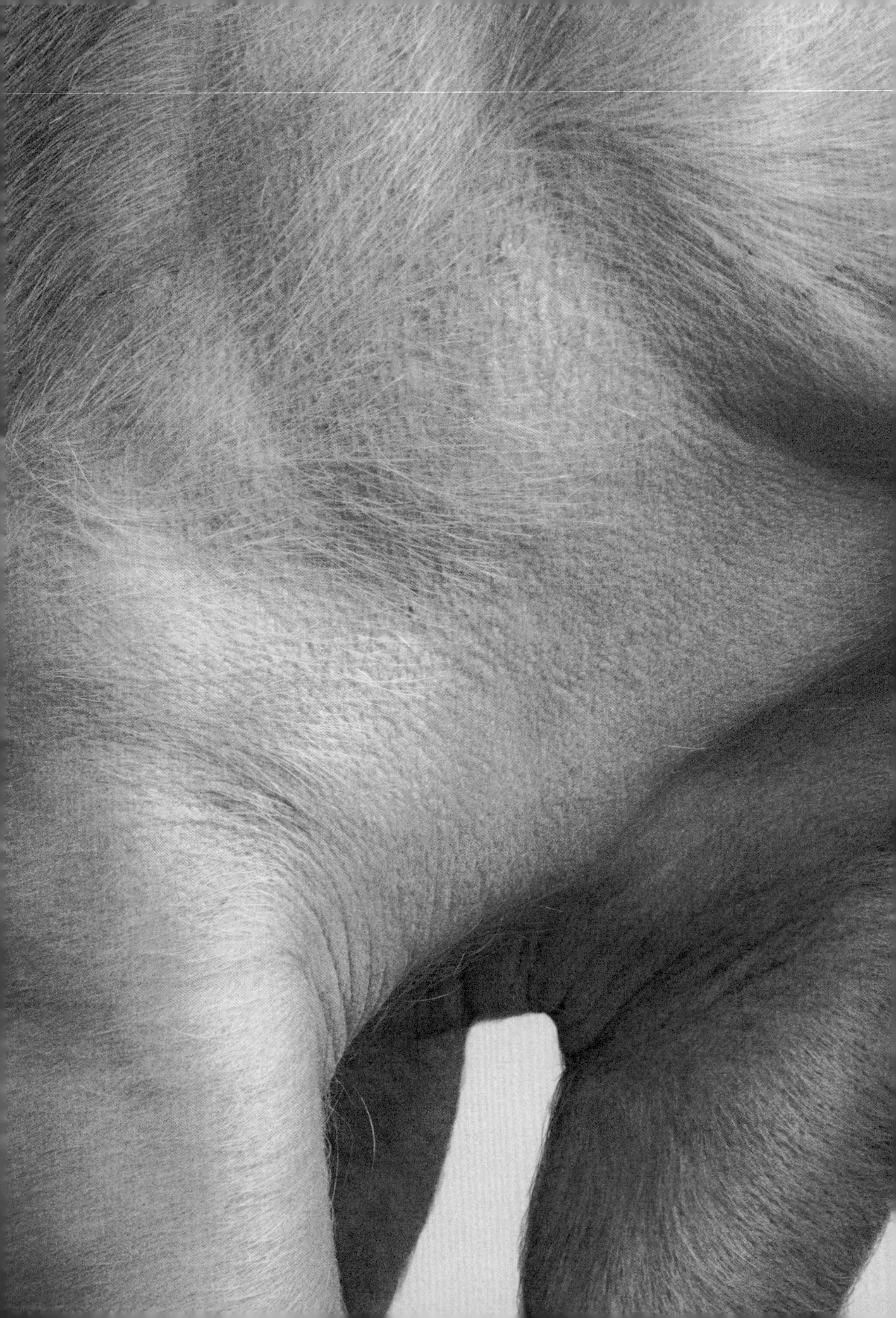

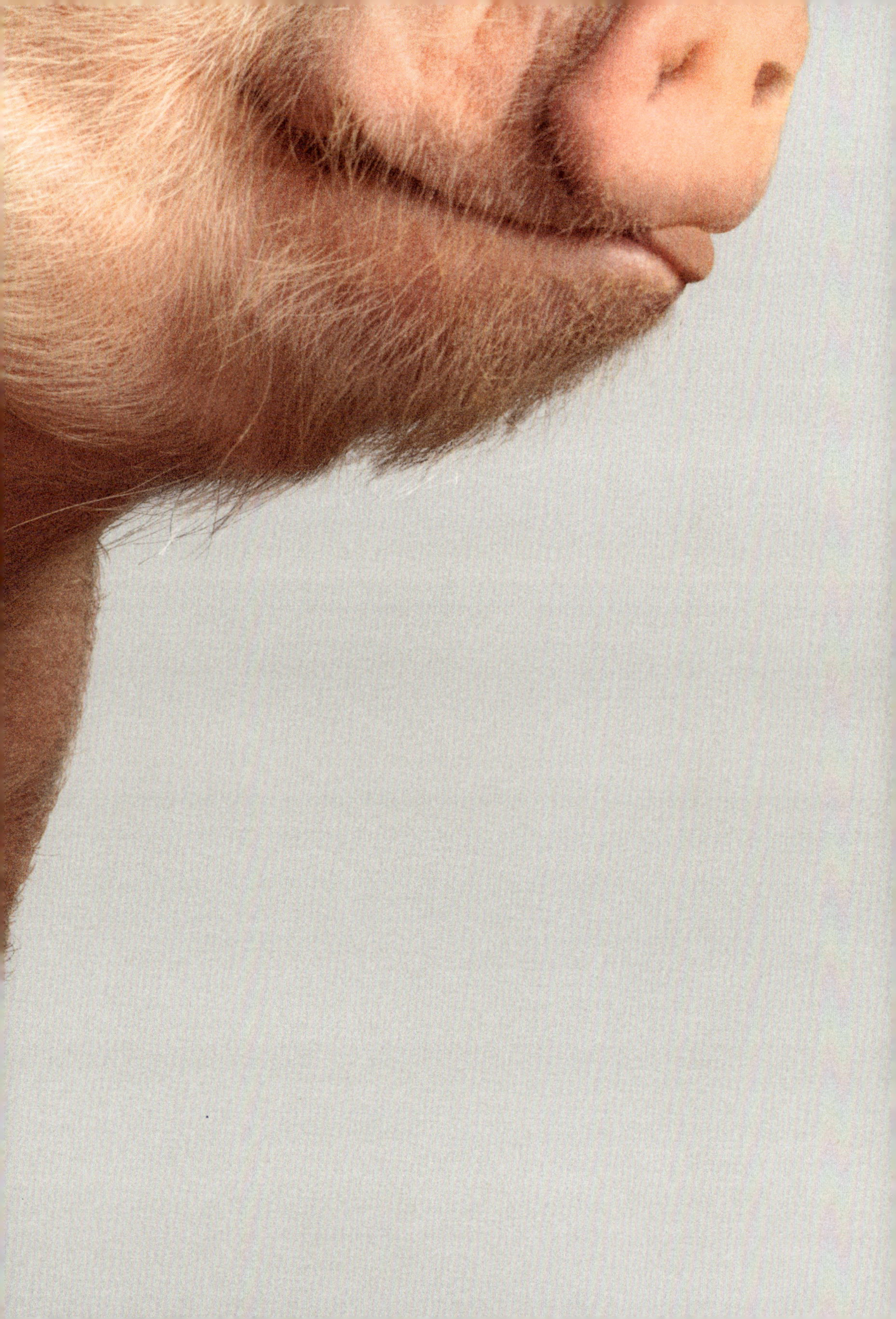

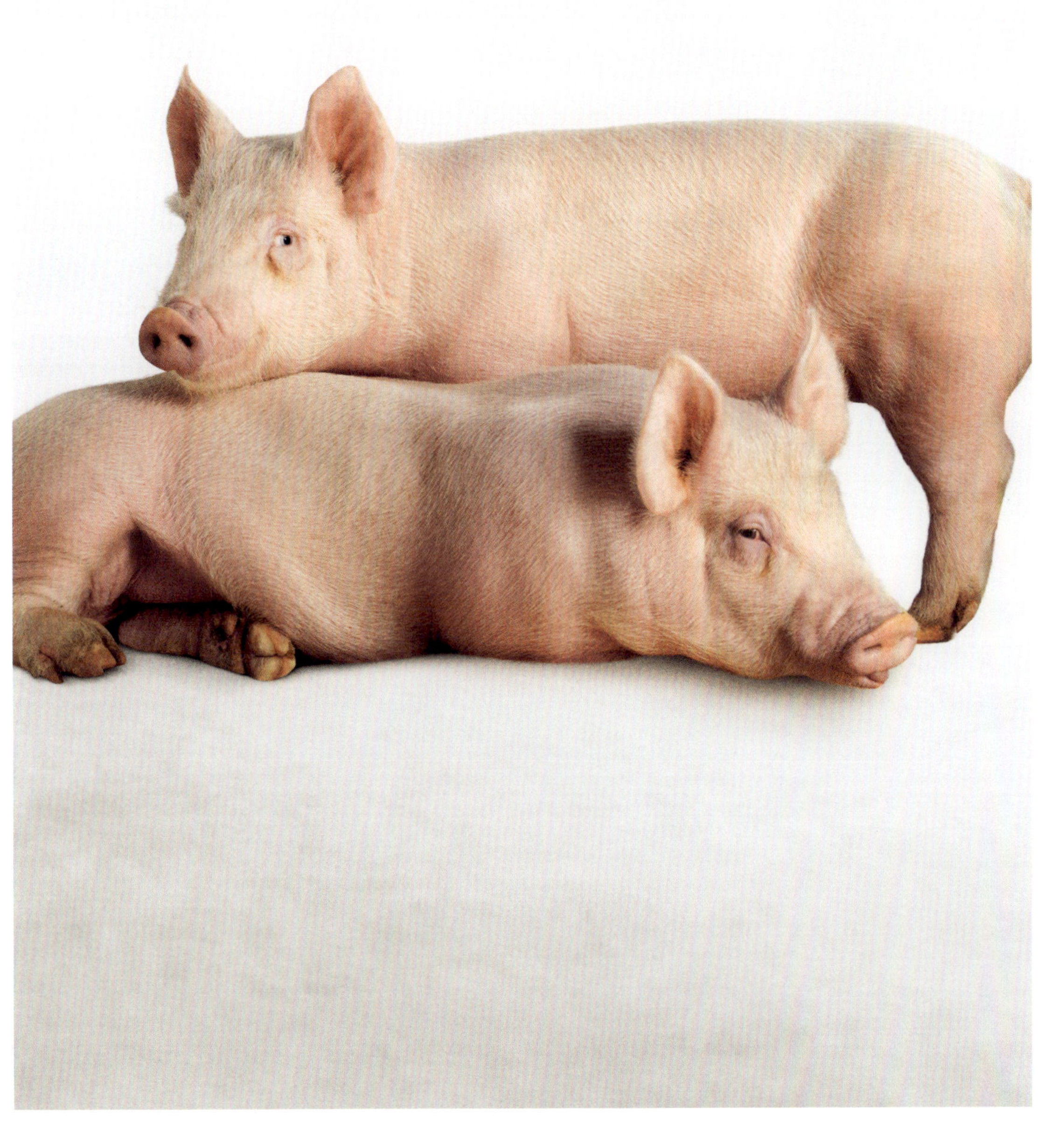

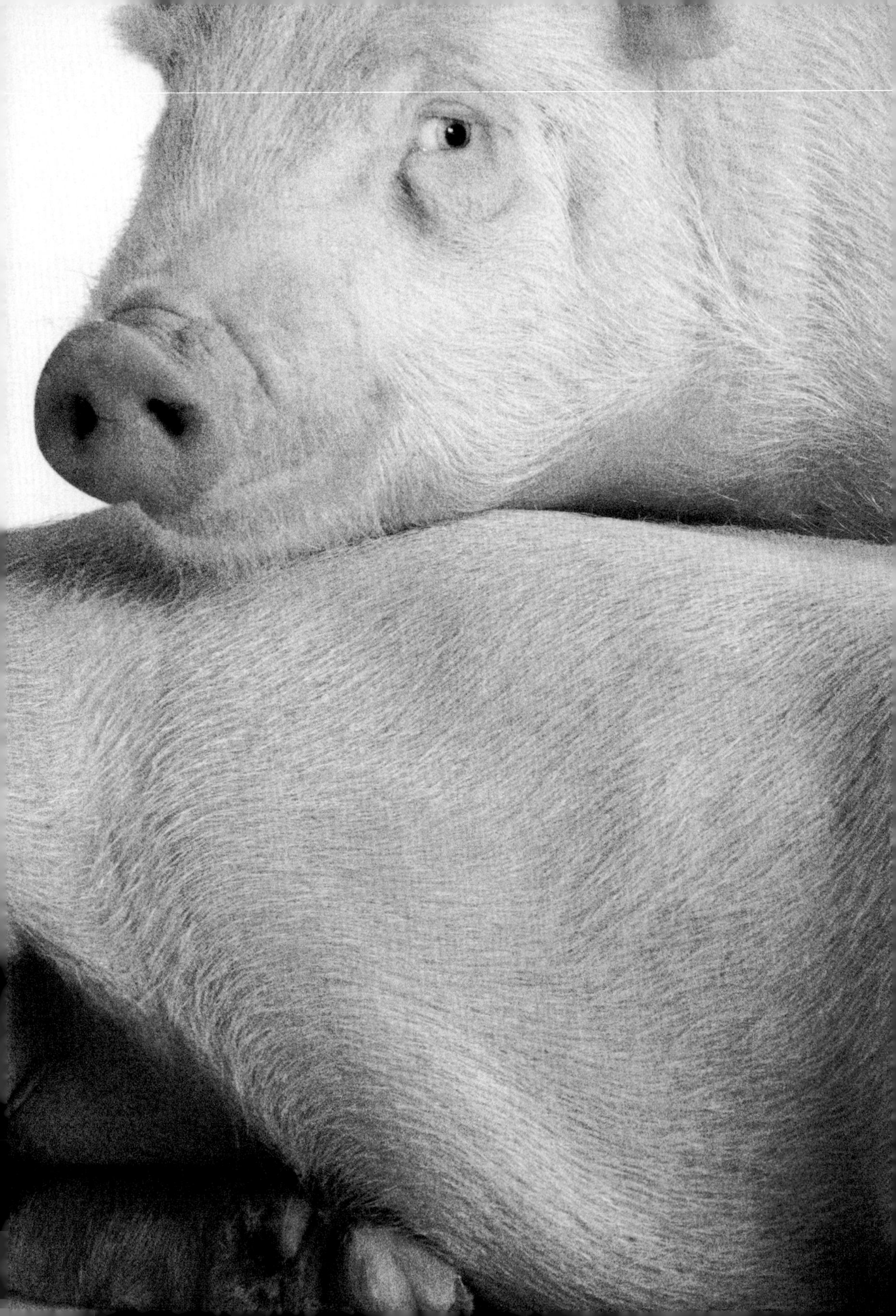

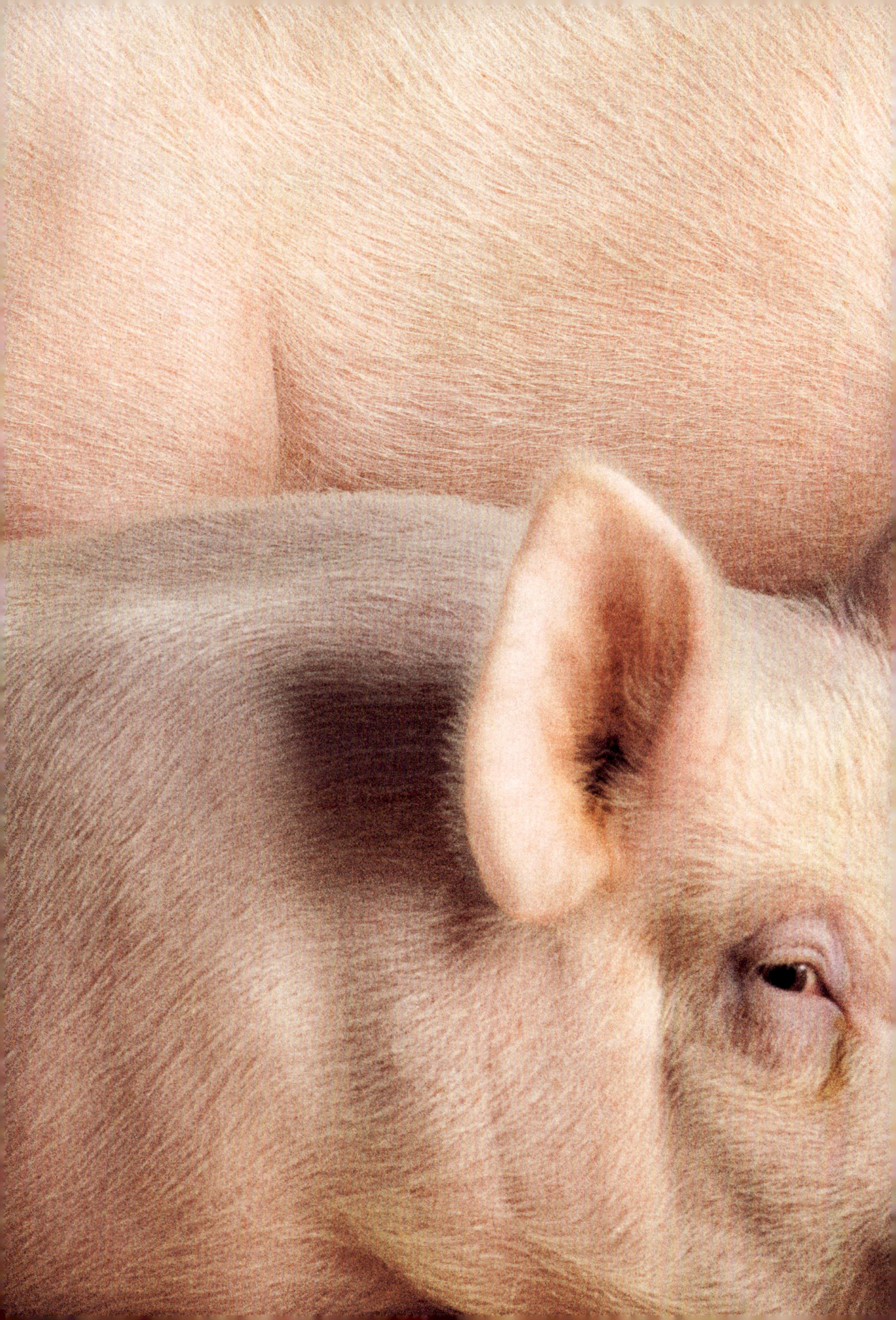

Big Nude I, 2023

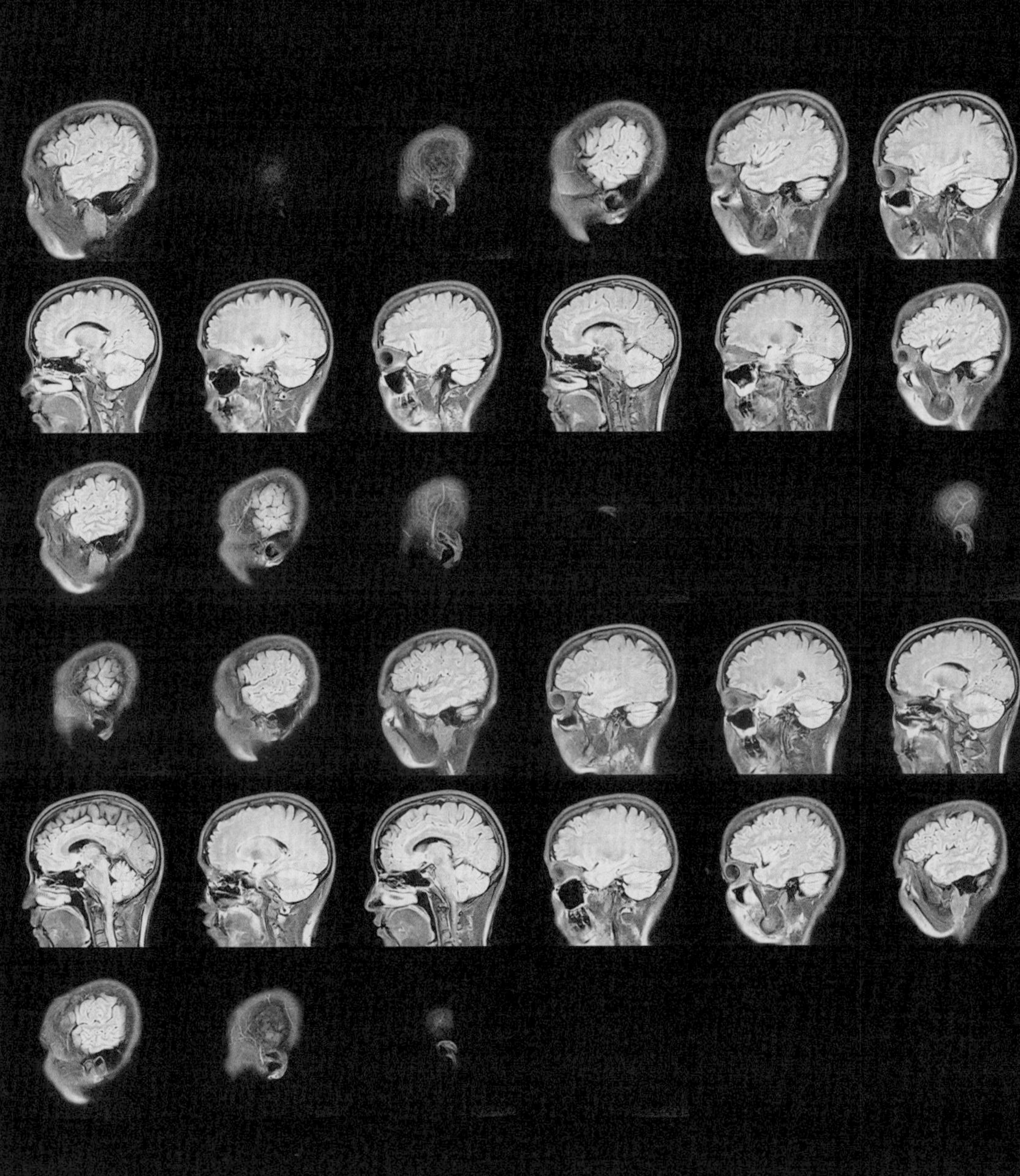

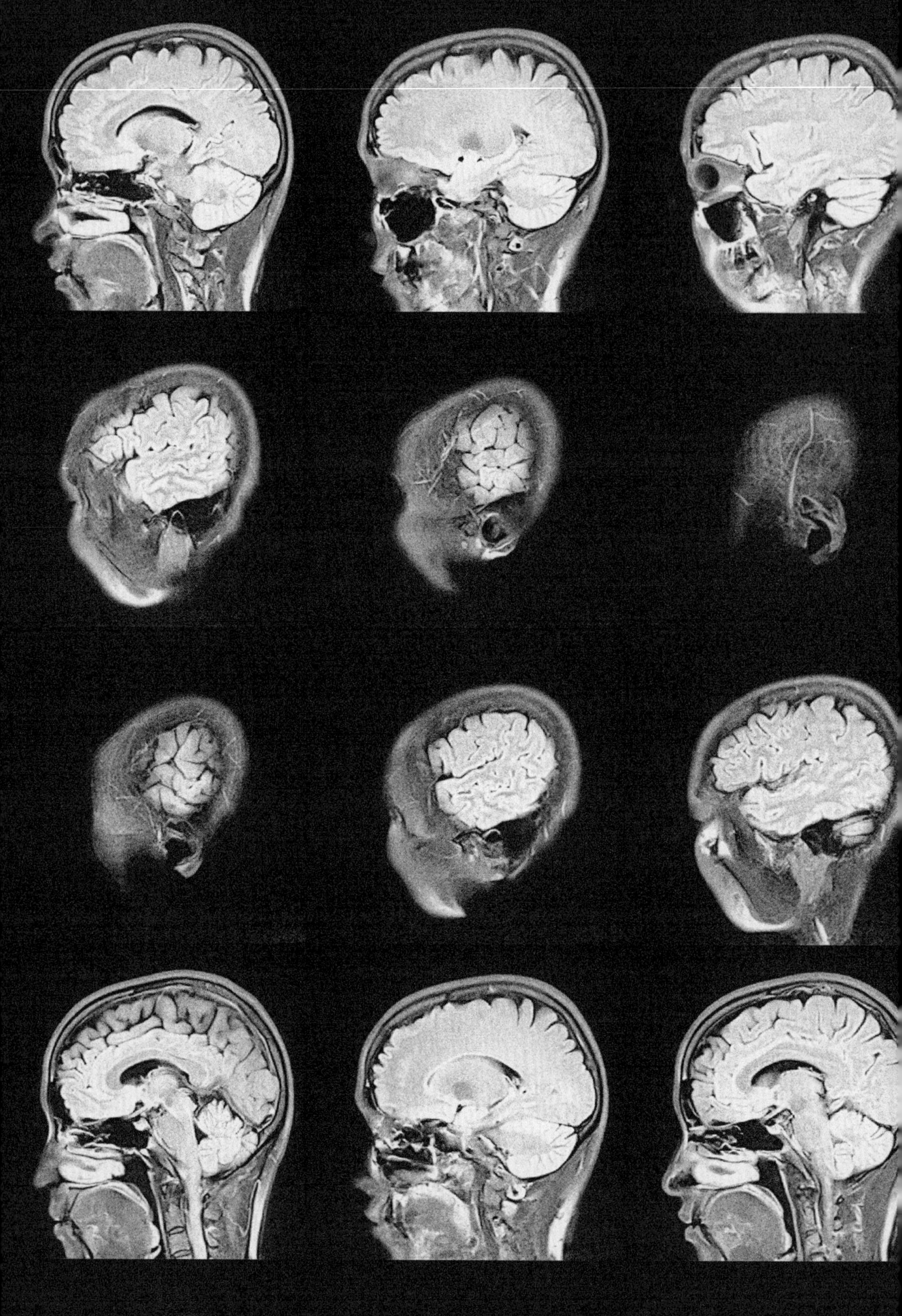

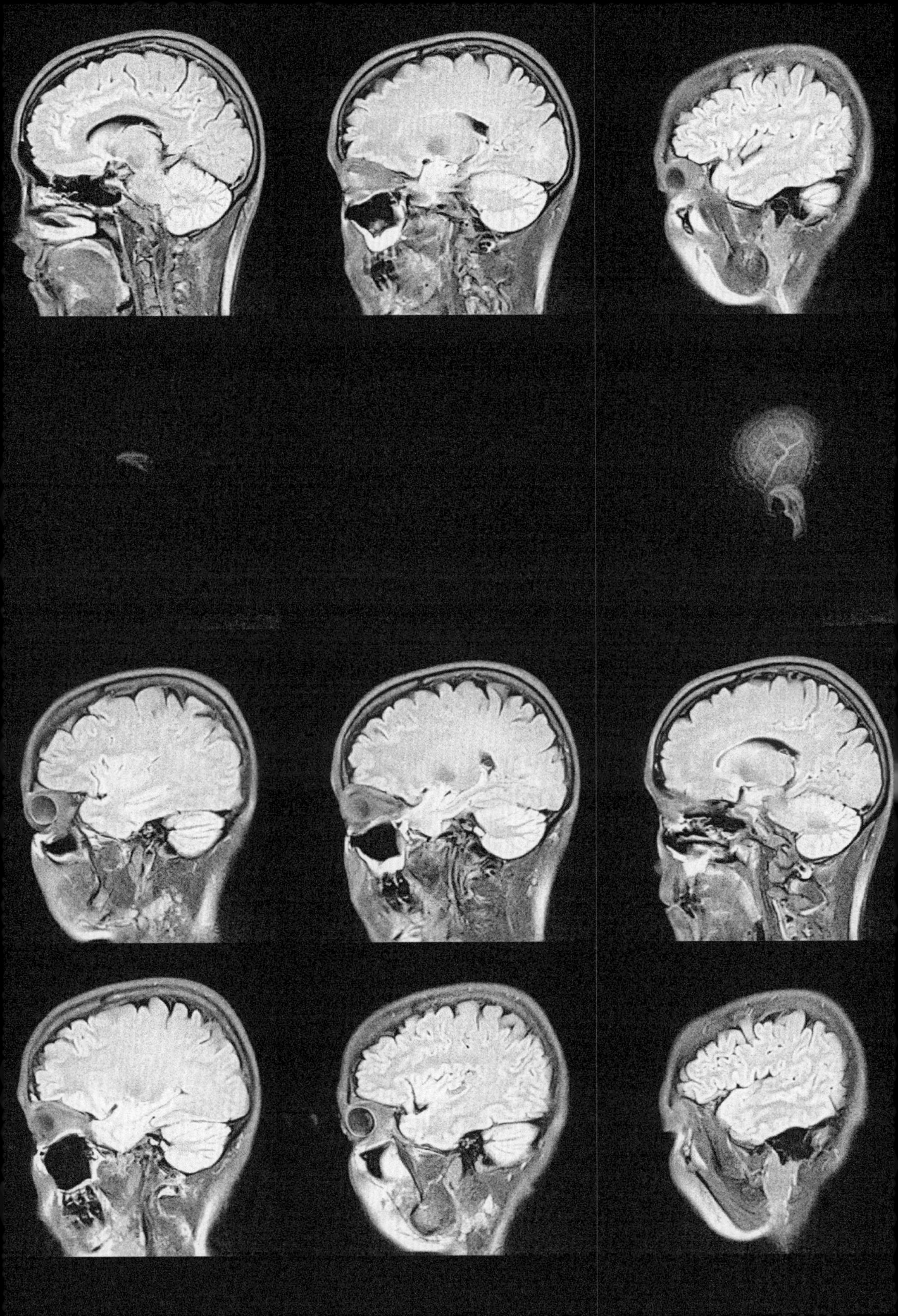

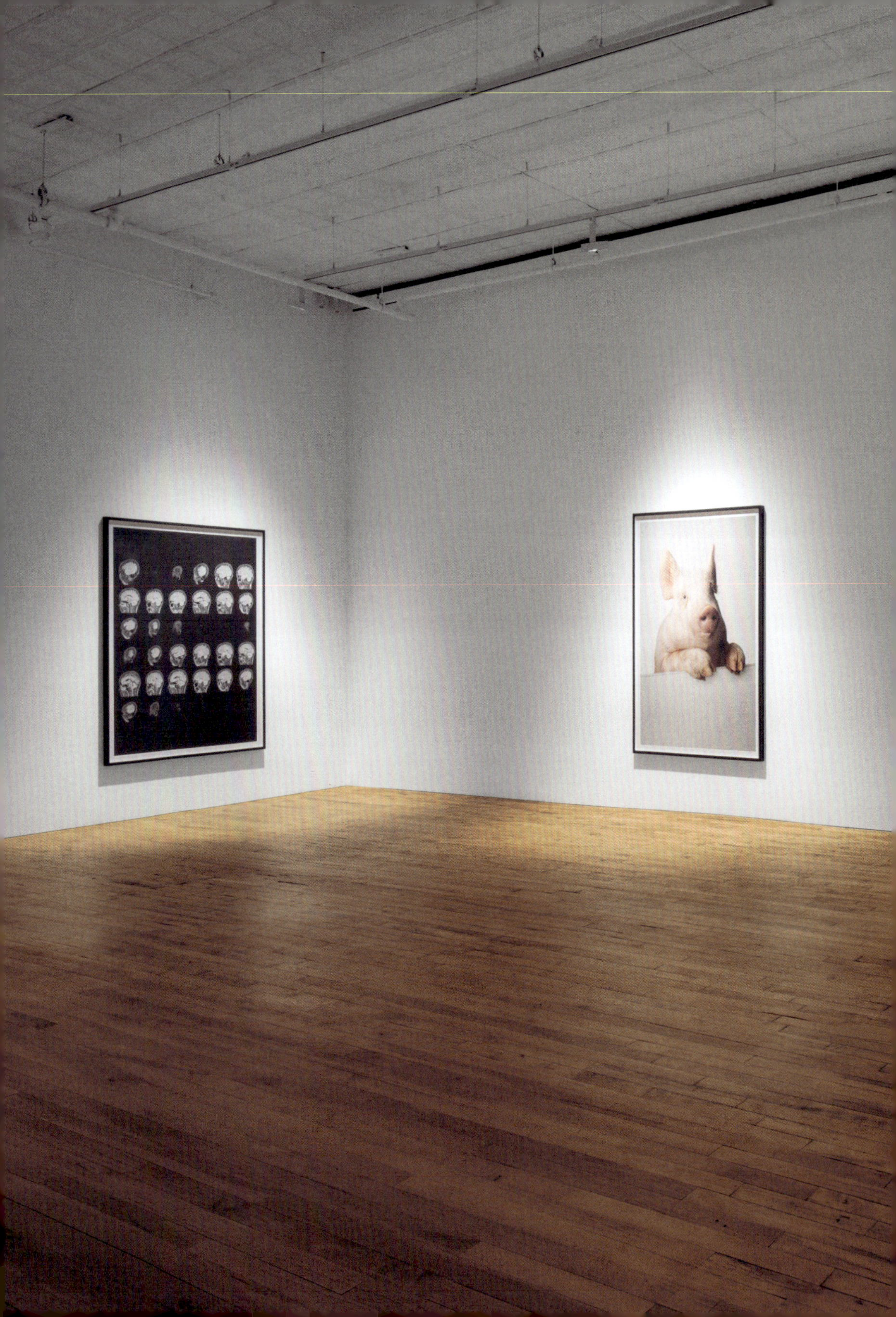

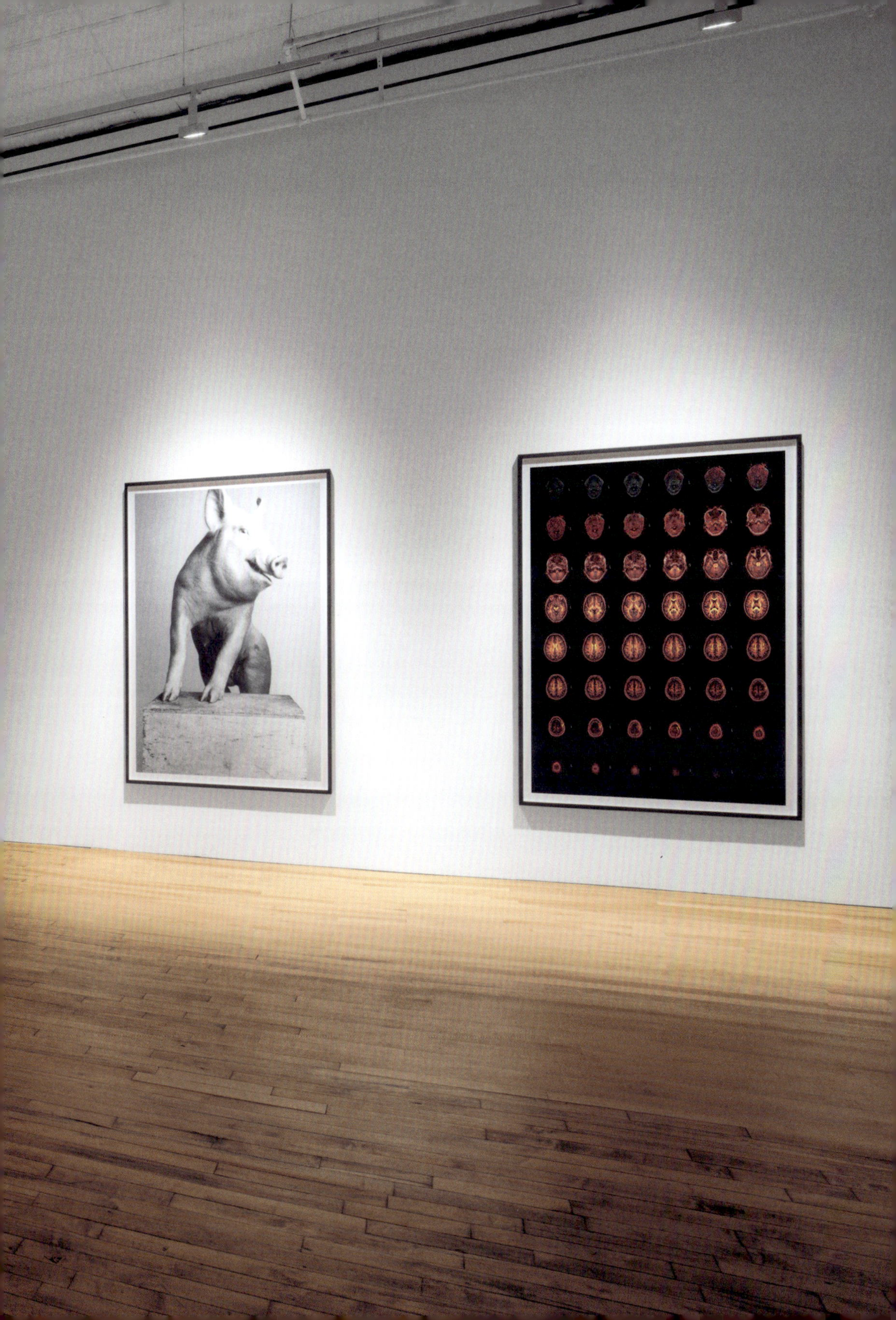

Derek, 2023

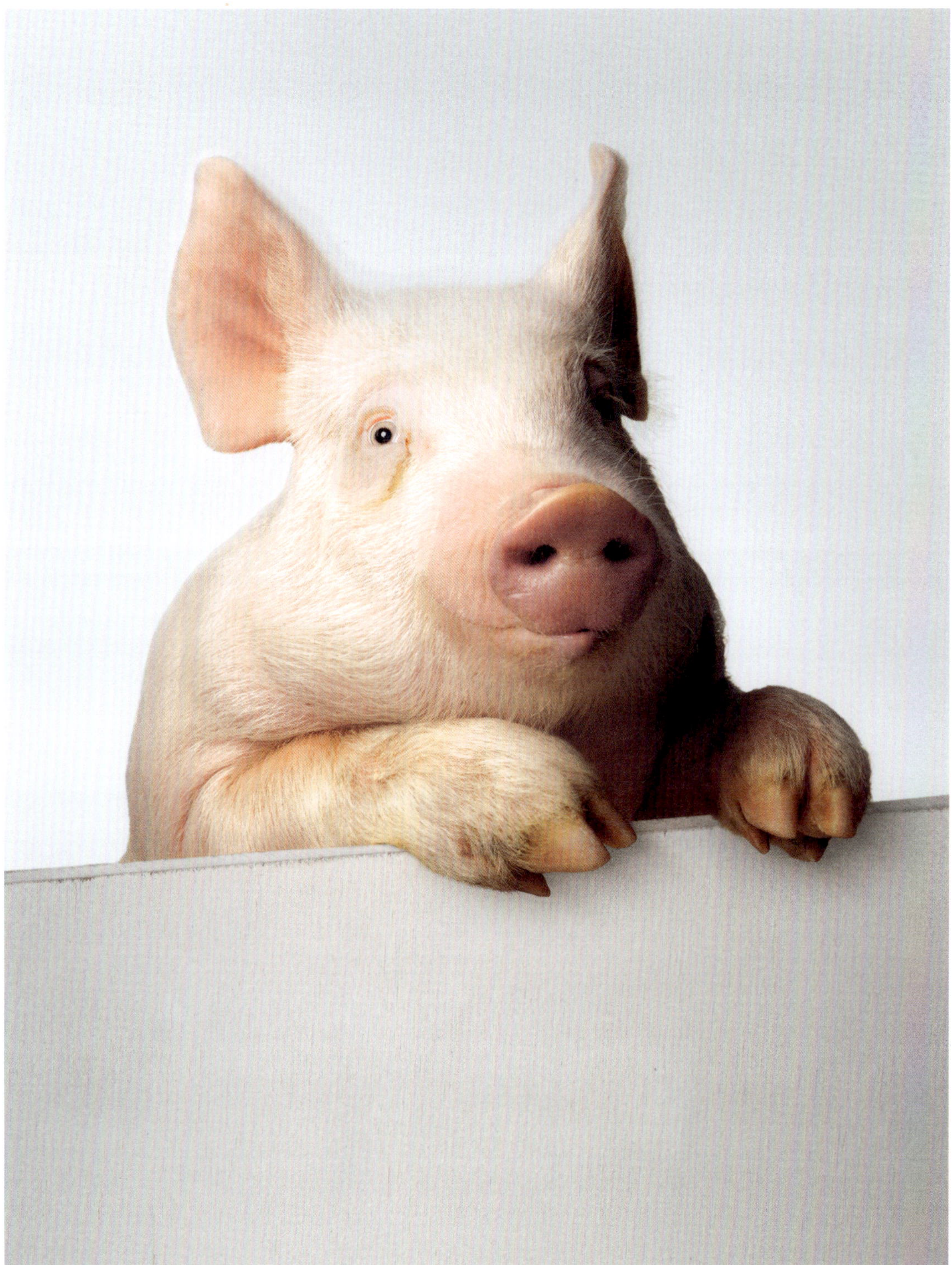

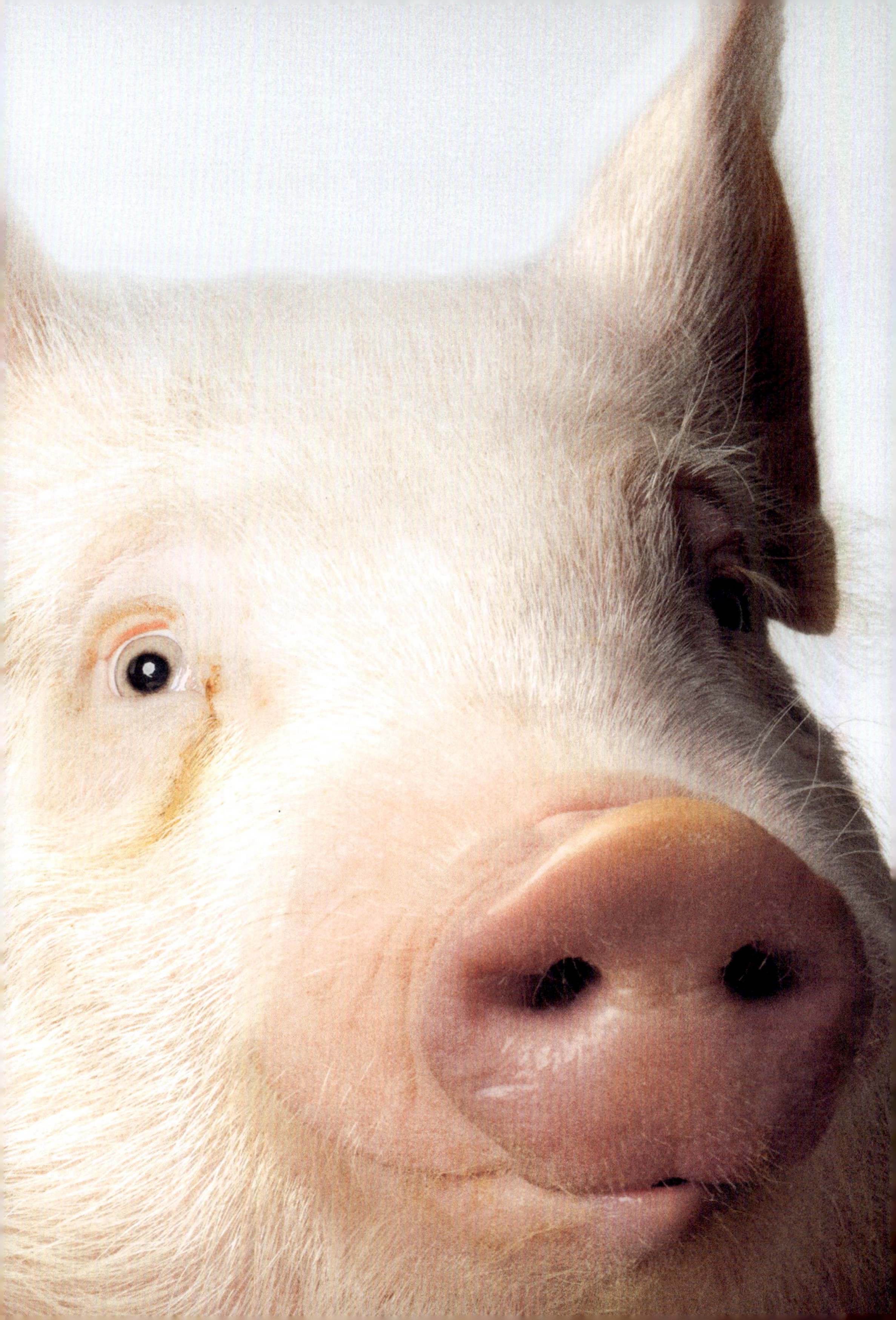

Butch, 2023

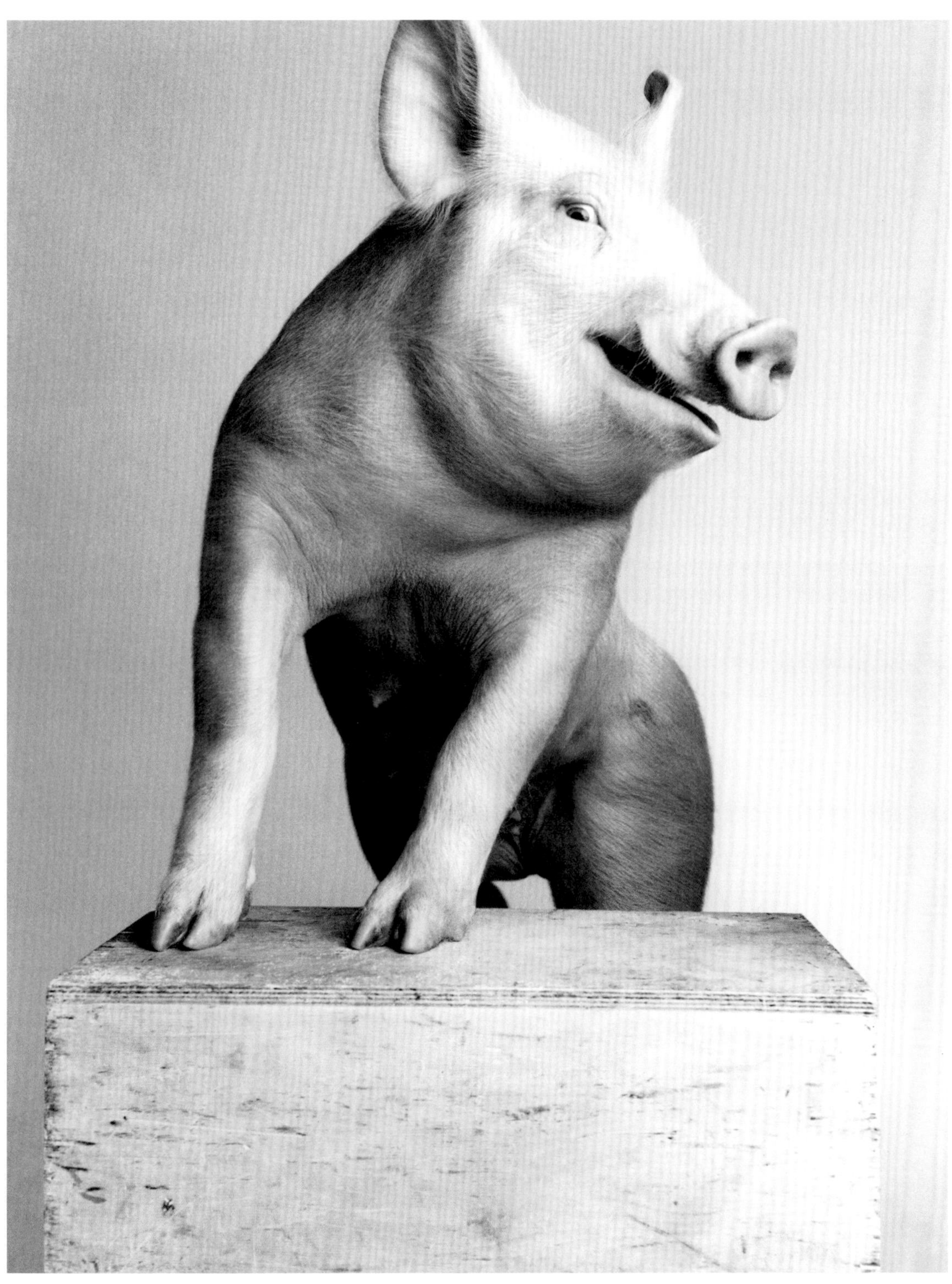

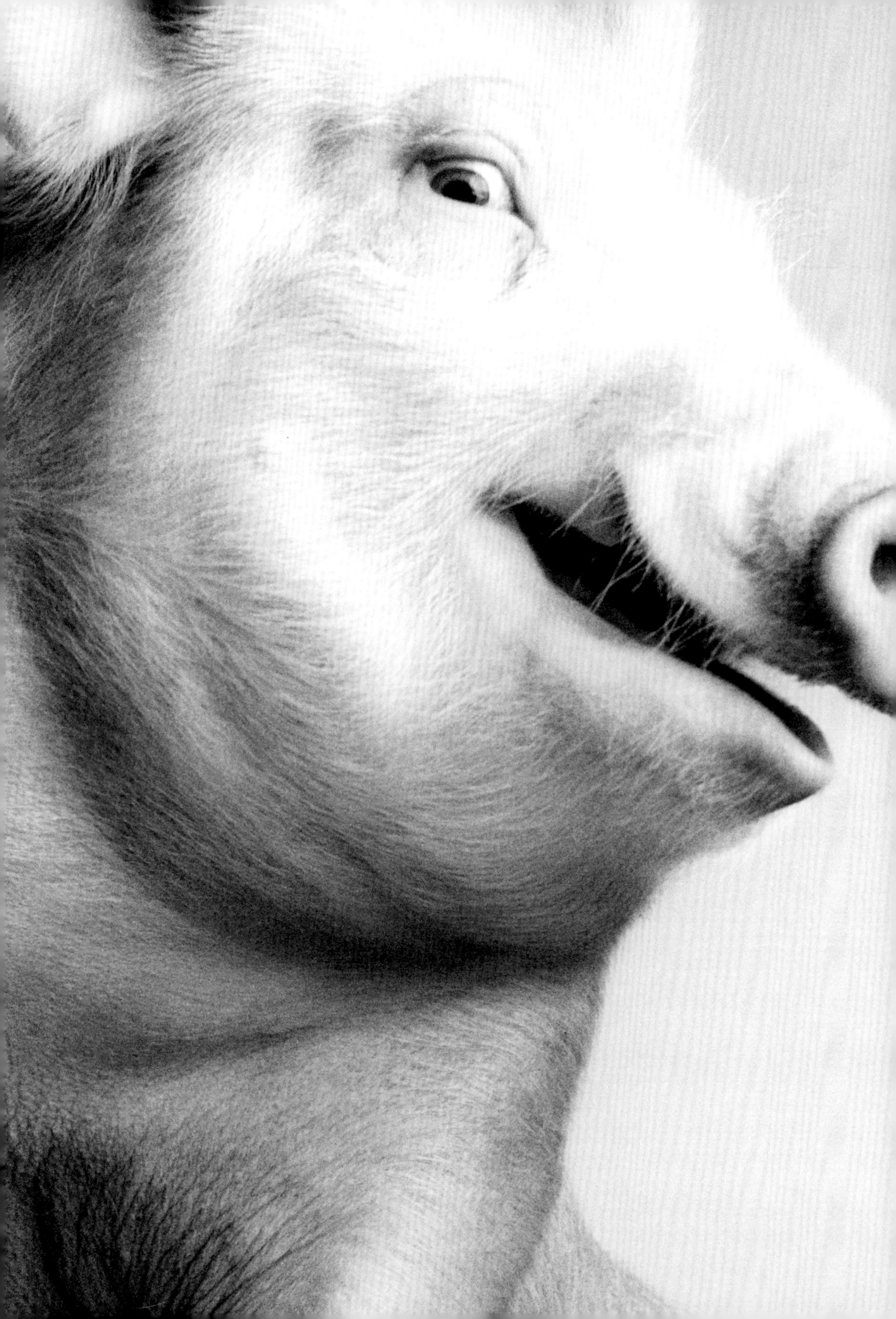

Big Nude III, 2023

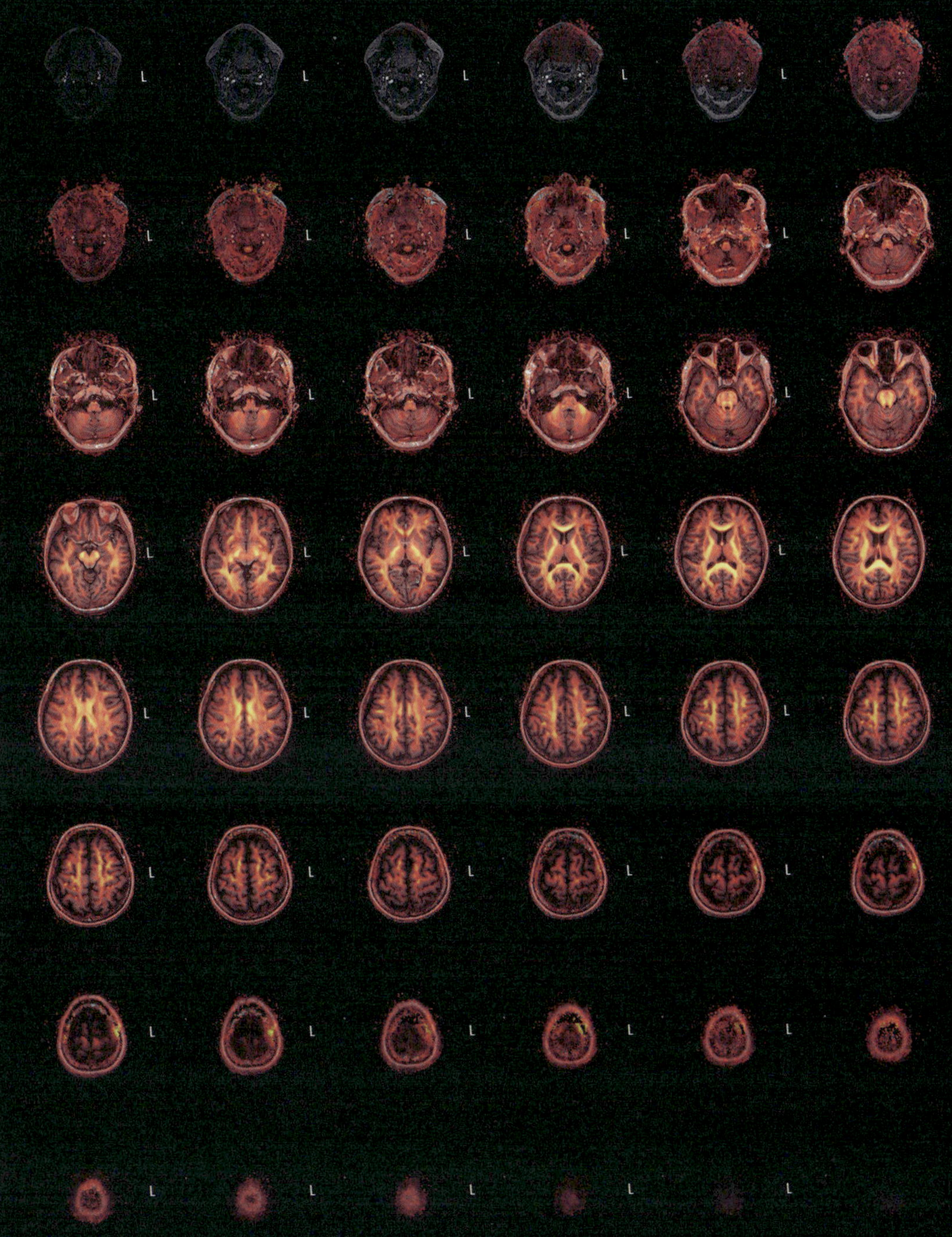

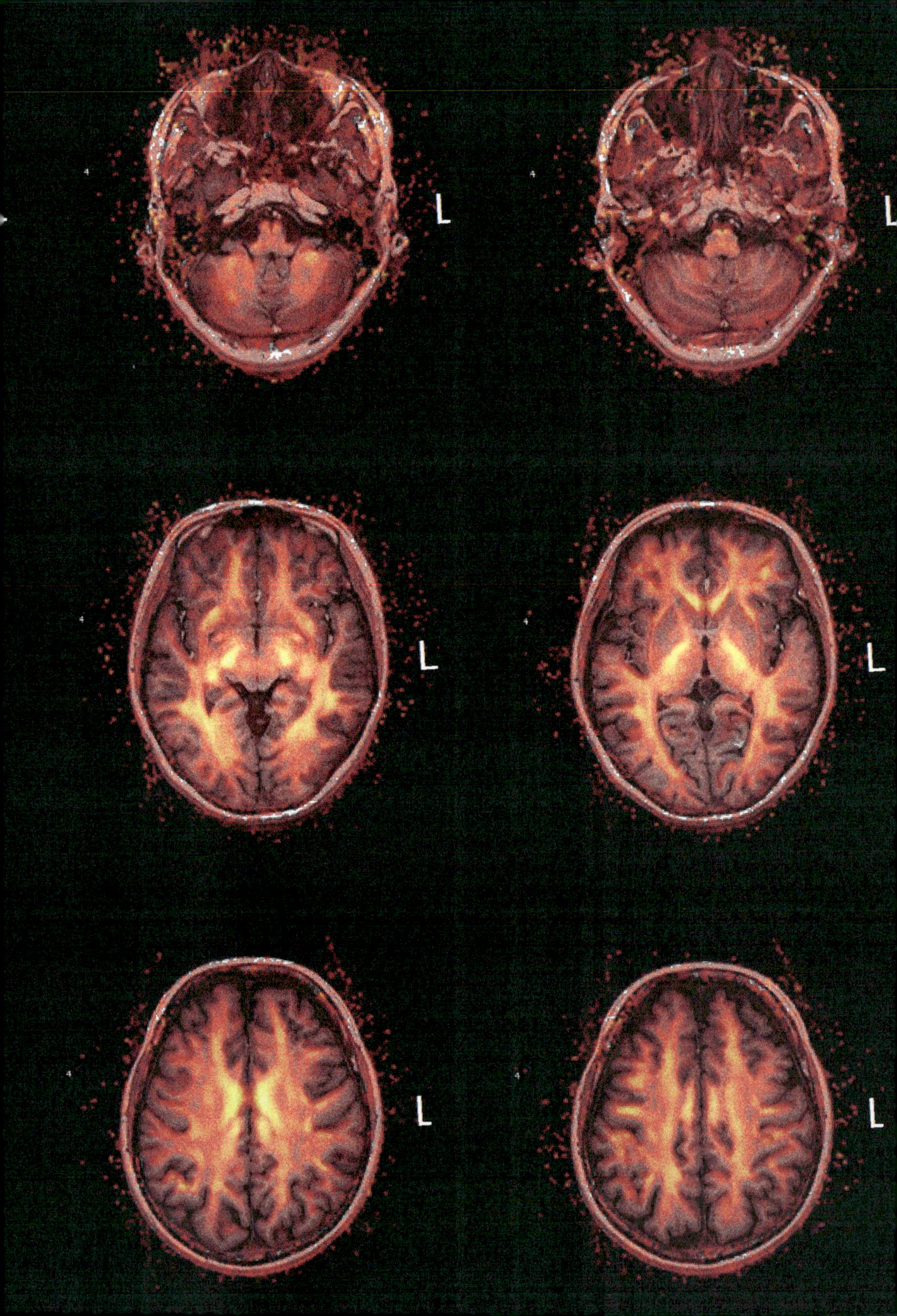
L
L
L
L
L
L

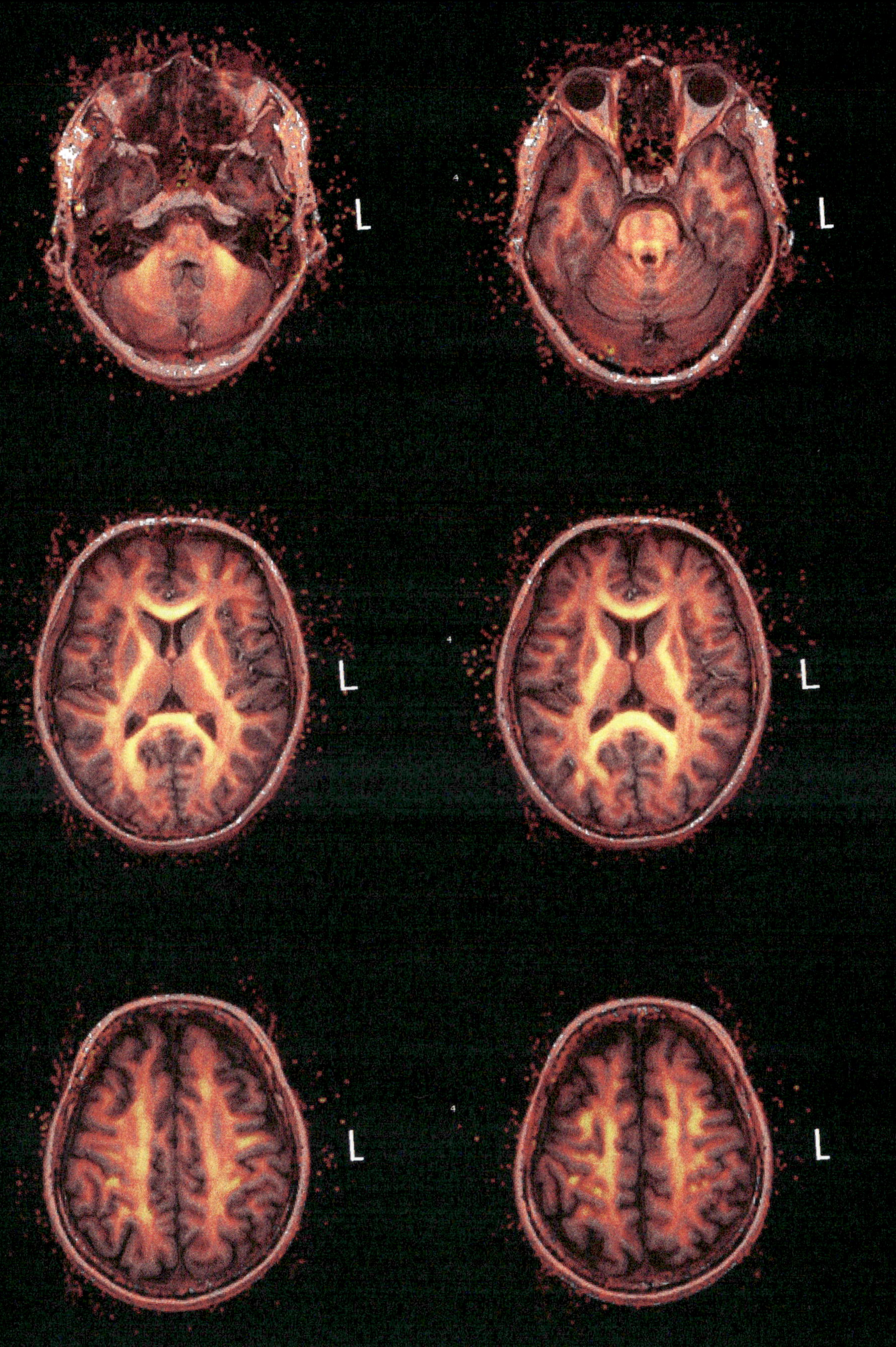
L
L
L
L
L
L

Figure Standing, 2023

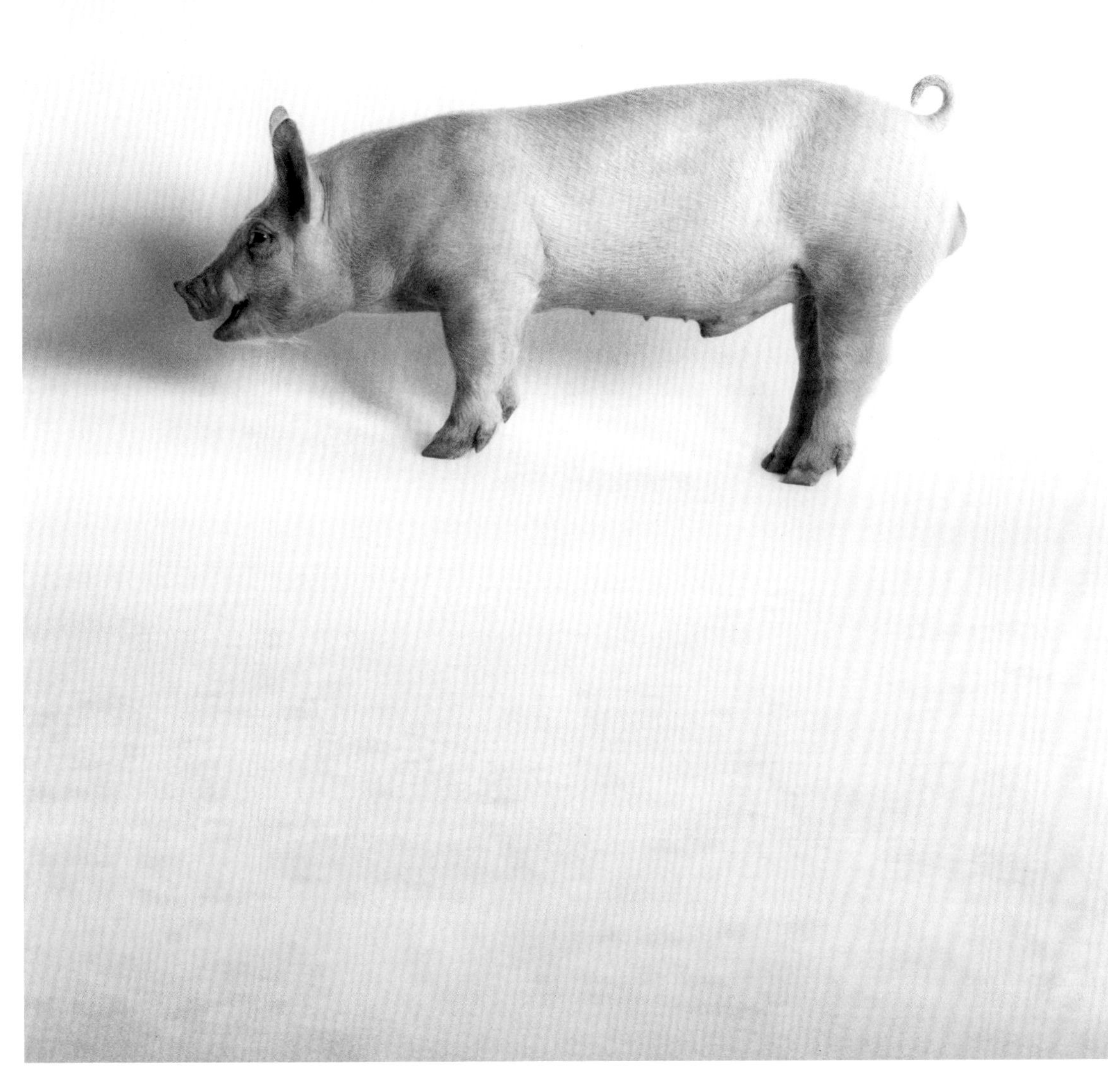

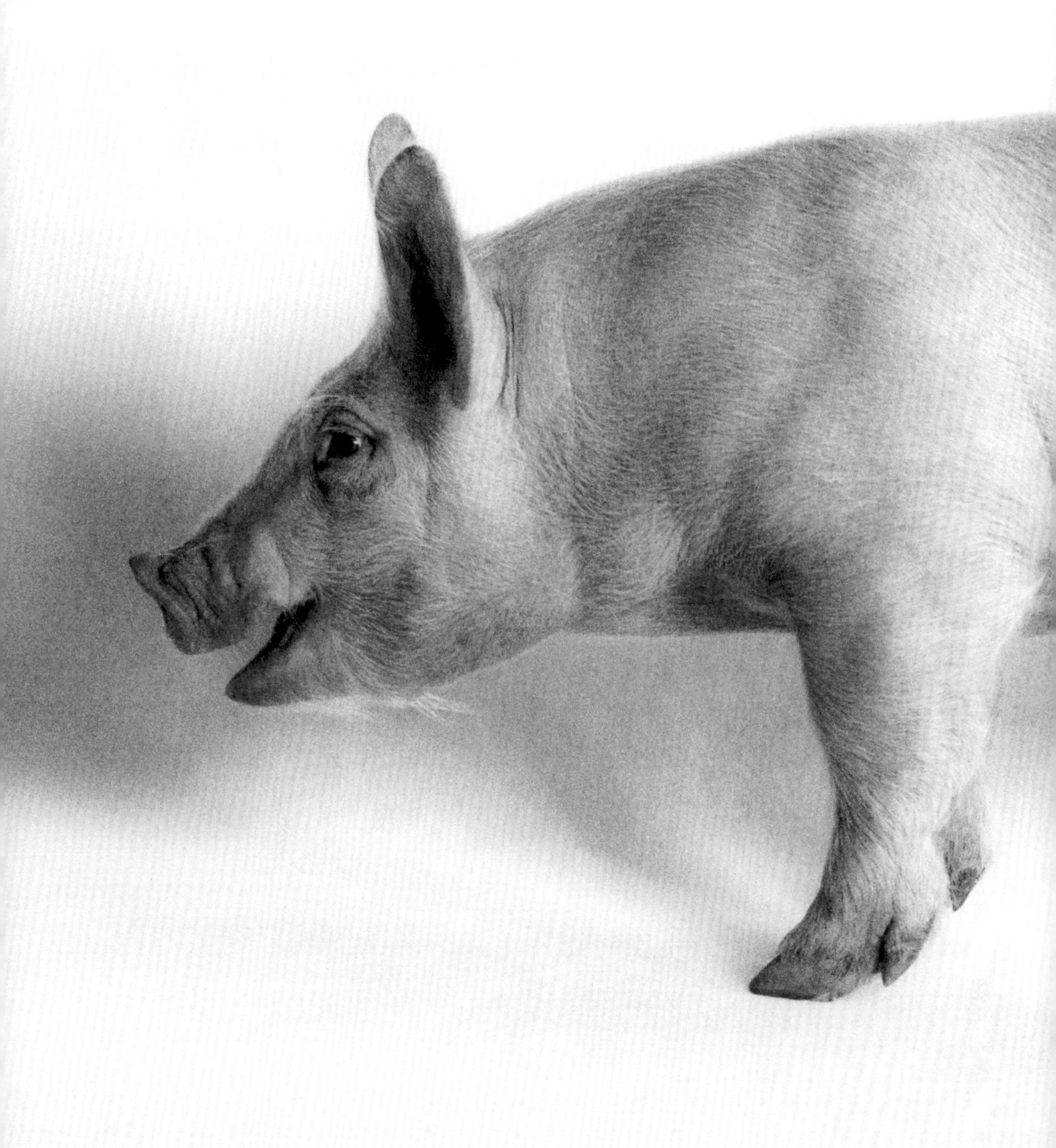

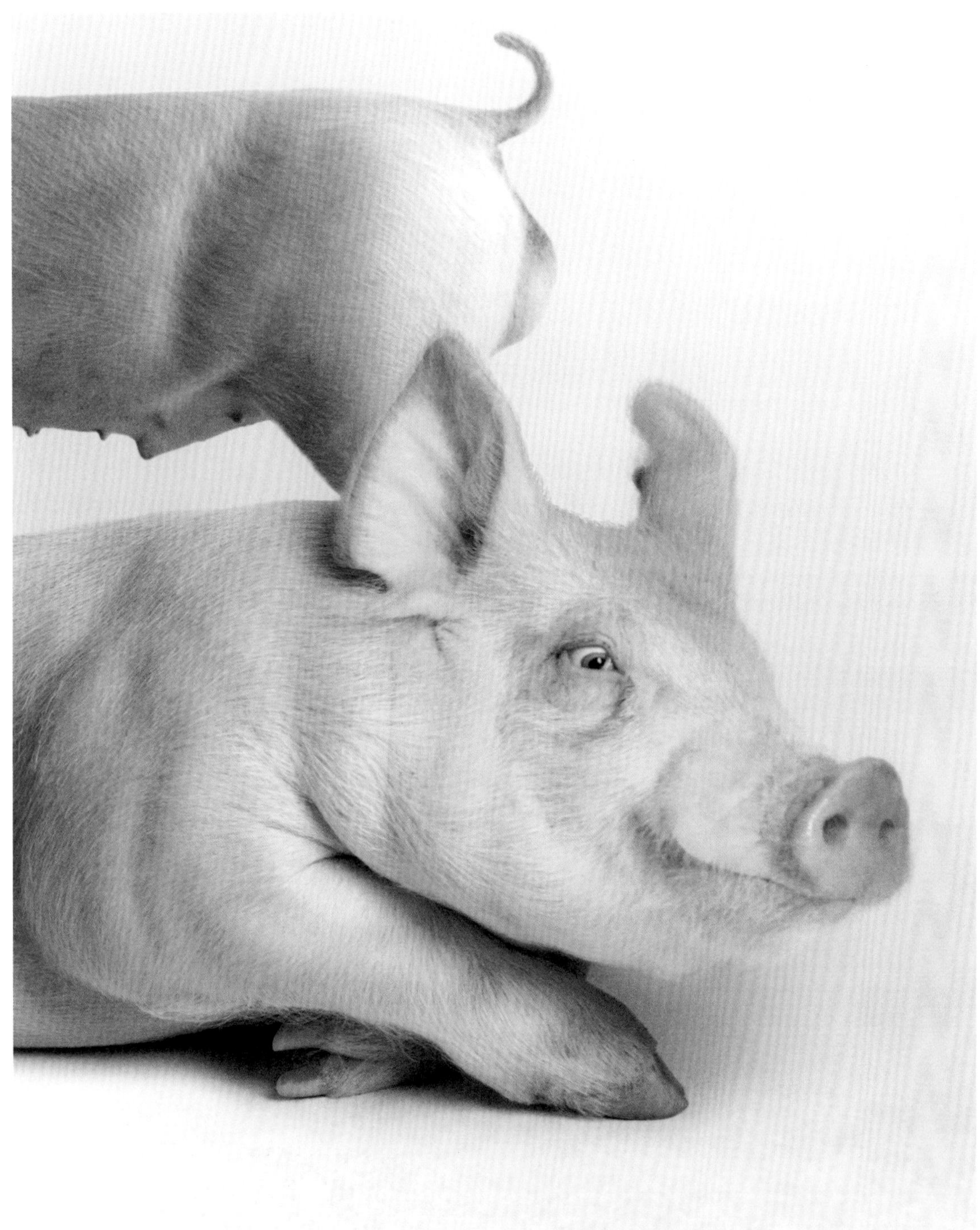

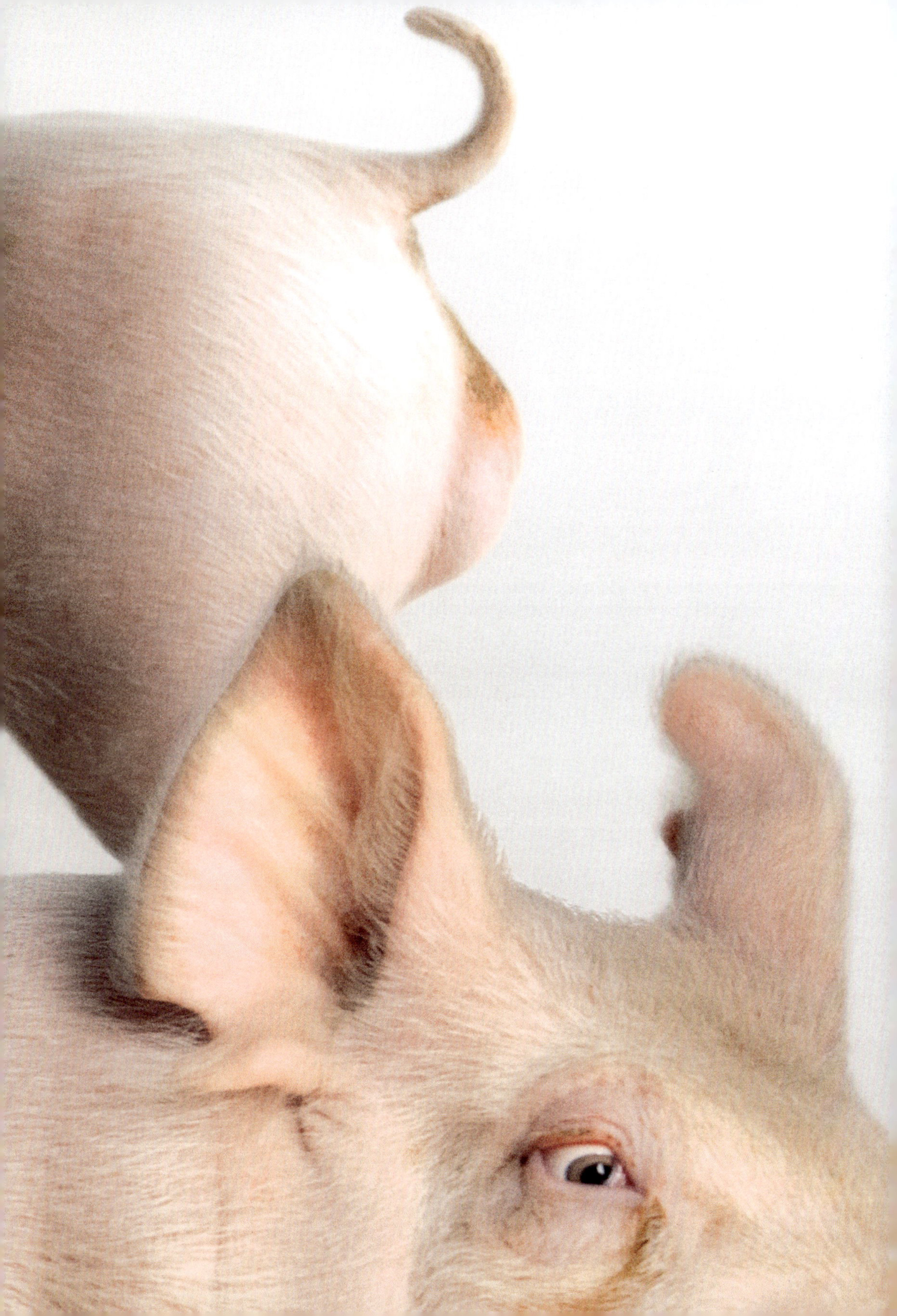

Big Nude I, 2023
Inkjet print
73 × 54 ¾ inches
185.4 × 139.1 cm
Page 55

Big Nude II, 2023
Inkjet print
73 × 54 ¾ inches
185.4 × 139.1 cm
Page 35

Big Nude III, 2023
Inkjet print
73 × 54 ¾ inches
185.4 × 139.1 cm
Page 69

Butch, 2023
Inkjet print
73 × 54 ¾ inches
185.4 × 139.1 cm
Page 65

Derek, 2023
Inkjet print
73 × 54 ¾ inches
185.4 × 139.1 cm
Page 61

Eat Me, 2023
Inkjet print
73 × 54 ¾ inches
185.4 × 139.1 cm
Page 31

Figure Standing, 2023
Inkjet print
73 × 54 ¾ inches
185.4 × 139.1 cm
Page 73

Matt and Chris, 2023
Inkjet print
73 × 54 ¾ inches
185.4 × 139.1 cm
Page 51

Reclining Nude, 2023
Inkjet print
73 × 54 ¾ inches
185.4 × 139.1 cm
Page 26

Sloth, 2023
Inkjet print
73 × 54 ¾ inches
185.4 × 139.1 cm
Page 47

Synchronicity, 2023
Inkjet print
73 × 54 ¾ inches
185.4 × 139.1 cm
Page 77

Untitled, 2023
Holographic installation; glass, pedestal, and four
flat-screen TVs
66 × 68 ⅛ × 68 ¼ inches
167.6 × 173 × 173.4 cm
Pages 38–43

You've come a long way, baby!, 2023
Inkjet print
73 × 54 ¾ inches
185.4 × 139.1 cm
Page 23

David Zwirner and Ebony L. Haynes wish to thank Heji Shin, without whom this exhibition and publication would not have been possible. Our thanks are also due to Benoît Lamy de La Chapelle for his illuminating text.

For their work on the exhibition, we are grateful to Rebecca Ashby-Colón, Cleo Bosmans, Susan Cernek, Jenny Cheng, Allison Chipak, Karryl Eugene, Maris Hutchinson, Felice Jiang, Jordan Kelly, Coco Kim, Julia Lukacher, David McBride, Jena Myung, Haley Darya Parsa, Julian Phillips, Erin Pinover, Nicholas Quint, Robert Richburg, Gabriela Scopazzi, Virginia Stroh, and Nora Woodin.

Thank you to Andrea Hyde for the catalogue series design and, for their work on this volume, to Bonnie Briant, Sergio Brunelli, Luke Chase, Fabio Ferrandini, Zeno Ferrandini, Doro Globus, Elizabeth Gordon, Jessica Palinski Hoos, Daniela Ioan, Avery Moore, Mari Perina, Chris Peterson, Molly Stein, Jules Thomson, Joey Young, and Lucas Zwirner.

The artist wishes to thank Aaron G. Filler, Jeff Goldenblum, Chris Medina, and Eric Van Valkenburg.

The *Clarion* series is an essential component of 52 Walker programming. An edition accompanies every exhibition, highlighting and expanding on the show's conceptual theses through newly commissioned texts, interviews, archival materials, and artistic interventions. The series is named in honor of the renowned author Octavia E. Butler, who was first published in the 1971 Clarion Science Fiction and Fantasy Writers' Workshop anthology.

Other Titles in the *Clarion* Series
I. Kandis Williams: A Line
II. Nikita Gale: END OF SUBJECT
III. Nora Turato: govern me harder
IV. Tiona Nekkia McClodden: MASK / CONCEAL / CARRY
V. Tau Lewis: Vox Populi, Vox Dei
VI. Gordon Matta-Clark & Pope.L: Impossible Failures
VII. Bob Thompson: So let us all be citizens

Forthcoming Titles
IX. Kayode Ojo: EDEN
X. Cauleen Smith: The Wanda Coleman Songbook

Published by 52 Walker and
David Zwirner Books
on the occasion of

Heji Shin: THE BIG NUDES
52 Walker, New York
July 21–October 7, 2023

52 Walker
52 Walker Street
New York, New York 10013
+1 212 727 1961
52walker.com

David Zwirner Books
520 West 20th Street, 2nd Floor
New York, New York 10011
+1 212 727 2070
davidzwirnerbooks.com

Editor: Ebony L. Haynes
Project editor: Jessica Palinski Hoos
Proofreader: Chris Peterson

Clarion series design: Andrea Hyde
Layout: Bonnie Briant
Photography coordination: Rebecca Ashby-Colón,
    Virginia Stroh
Production manager: Luke Chase
Color separations: VeronaLibri, Verona
Printing: VeronaLibri, Verona

Typefaces: DTL Fleischmann, Genath
Paper: Magno Natural, 140 gsm

Publication © 2025 52 Walker and David Zwirner Books

"Curator's Note: A Pig Walks into a Bar…"
    © 2025 Ebony L. Haynes
"Squealing like a Pig" © 2025 Benoît Lamy de La Chapelle

All artwork by Heji Shin © 2025 Heji Shin

Photography
All installation views were photographed by Maris Hutchinson.

p. 10: © Jeff Koons
pp. 12 (all), 14: Courtesy Heji Shin and Reena Spauldings
Fine Art, New York/Los Angeles

The work on page 77 was not included in the exhibition at
52 Walker, New York.

Distributed in the United States and Canada by
Simon & Schuster, Inc.
1230 Avenue of the Americas
New York, New York 10020
simonandschuster.com

Distributed outside the United States and Canada by
Thames & Hudson, Ltd.
181A High Holborn
London WC1V 7QX
thamesandhudson.com

ISBN 978-1-64423-139-5

Library of Congress Control Number: 2024942948

Printed in Italy

Notes

Notes

Notes